To Allan: from one story teller to another.

FAT & FUNNY

(So, you want to be Santa Claus)

Michael Supe Granda

Michael Supe Granda

authorHOUSE

AuthorHouse™
1663 Liberty Drive
Bloomington, IN 47403
www.authorhouse.com
Phone: 833-262-8899

© 2022 Michael Supe Granda. All rights reserved.

No part of this book may be reproduced, stored in a retrieval system, or transmitted by any means without the written permission of the author.

Published by AuthorHouse   07/26/2022

ISBN: 978-1-6655-5478-7 (sc)
ISBN: 978-1-6655-5477-0 (hc)
ISBN: 978-1-6655-5451-0 (e)

Library of Congress Control Number: 2022905025

Print information available on the last page.

Any people depicted in stock imagery provided by Getty Images are models, and such images are being used for illustrative purposes only. Certain stock imagery © Getty Images.

This book is printed on acid-free paper.

Because of the dynamic nature of the Internet, any web addresses or links contained in this book may have changed since publication and may no longer be valid. The views expressed in this work are solely those of the author and do not necessarily reflect the views of the publisher, and the publisher hereby disclaims any responsibility for them.

Contents

Acknowledgments vii

Foreword ix

Introduction xi

Chapter 1   Resumé 1

Chapter 2   The First Glimpse 8

Chapter 3   Breakfast with Santa 16

Chapter 4   Your First Gig 21

Chapter 5   Minty Breath 29

Chapter 6   Pretty Flowers 38

Chapter 7   Santa Meter 44

Chapter 8   Small-Town Friday Night 52

Chapter 9   Lists 59

Chapter 10 Santa goes to the Ballet 67

Chapter 11 House Concerts 76

Chapter 12 Mrs. Claus 84

Chapter 13 Older Gals Like Santa, Too 91

Chapter 14 Double Duty and Double D's 98

Chapter 15 Santa goes to Christian College 109

Chapter 16 Santa Hits the Gridiron 116

Chapter 17 Not Every Moment Is Golden 127

Chapter 18   Pirates, Ornaments, and Garbonzos................ 134

Chapter 19   You Are What You Eat....................................... 152

Chapter 20   Out of the Suit... 160

Chapter 21   Flirting with Santa 171

Chapter 22   The Last Waltz... 177

Chapter 23   Epilogue 185

Photo Credits 187

About the Author 189

Acknowledgments

I'd like to thank a few folks, who have been instrumental in helping to get this Santa gig off the ground and moving along.

A heartfelt thanks to Carol Buttenham, who saw my Santa shtick, recognized the potential, and began booking me around town.

To the Tennessee Titans, the Nashville Ballet, the Butter Cake Babe Coffee Café, and the Country Music Hall of Fame for allowing me to perform on their stages.

To Tom Mason and his Blue Buccaneers for allowing me to "Ho, ho, ho" alongside his "Yo, ho, ho."

To Jen Gunderman and her Ornaments for allowing me to join in and do my lame duck walk across their stage.

To Chris Slatinsky and John Ehlers for their Garbonzo approach to music and life.

To Buddy Dow and Eve Ardell at AuthorHouse for their advice and guidance.

To Stacie Huckeba, Mickey Dobo, Casey Lutton, James White, Steve Harman, Kevin Wisniewski, Jamie Rubin, and Madison Thorn for their photographic eyes.

To Mark Horn for hosting his family gatherings, where I began to hone my Santa chops, as well as being Santa's drummer and banjo player.

To Peter Cooper for his kind words in the newspaper and his recommendation to the hall.

To my wife, Julie, who chuckles every time I put on the red suit and head off into the world, but recognizes the legitimacies of my side gig.

To the malls, schools, community centers, churches, and businesses who have allowed me to thrill and tickle their youngsters.

Last, I'd like to thank all the children, young and old, who have allowed me into their gaze and into their lives, as Santa. You have helped me keep a young heart in this old chest.

Peace on earth and goodwill to humankind.

Foreword

Okay, Michael 'Supe' Granda is a lovable, smart (really smart), funny, clever, creative entity. As the bass player and one of the driving forces of the Ozark Mountain Daredevils is the way I first came to know him. Which is great enough, as it is. I even worked for them on a couple of shows as a late teen, when I worked with a sound company that did some shows with them. I was a skinny little creepy hippie, who lifted gear that weighed WAY more than I did. But I loved every minute of the couple of times I was in their presence. But, here's the thing. Supe is much more than a guy in a band. He keeps his spirit alive by constantly creating whatever pops into his head. He says he's an old fart, but he's eternally a goofy, wonderful kid. So, he's written this book. You gotta read this. If you're reading these words of mine here, you obviously have the book in your paws. Supe claims to not be fond of Christmas, but fond of Santa Claus. I don't believe it. I believe he's crazy about Santa and Christmas. I just think when you reach a certain age, you start to think you're supposed to say Bah Humbug!!! You'll love this book and Supe will take you on an interesting, funny, heartwarming journey into his (and Santy's) world. They are both good boys.

                                                Billy Bob Thornton, Bellflower, CA

Introduction

I thank you, dearly. I'm absolutely thrilled and honored that you've decided to pick up this book. It's going to be a fun ride, just like being Santa Claus.

This is not an instruction manual. There are no steps to follow. This is not a part of any kind of *Santa for Dummies* series.

These chapters are not really chapters, but experiences. They are not laid out in any specific sequence, nor were they written in any particular order. They came to me all at once—a literal tsunami of red. Each is a story about what I saw, did, looked at, laughed at, teared up at, and experienced at my gig that particular day.

Some recount actual gigs—the sights, the sounds, the

aromas, the folklore, the eggnog. Some are simple exposés on the craft of acting. After all, this is an acting gig. If you get the gig, you're just an actor portraying Santa Claus.

Ed Wynn portrayed Santa Claus. Ed Asner also portrayed Santa Claus. Art Carney, Billy Bob Thornton, and John Goodman all portrayed Santa Claus. If you wish, you can too.

If this book were a CD, I would instruct you to hit the "random" button on your player and let 'er rip. If you want to read chapter 18 before chapter 6, feel free. It will not hinder continuity, one bit. You may even see some of the same observations in several different places.

I hope you'll have as much fun reading about being an old, fat guy in a red suit, as I've had, being an old, fat guy in a red suit. Let me tell you—the old boy is a hoot. There is one big drawback, though. There is no such thing as a young, strapping Santa. Santa Claus is an old man. Those of us who portray him are old men. That's all there is to it. A fact is a fact. There's no getting around it.

And what is the main thing old men dread? Why, that would be kicking the bucket. One day, I will. One day, you will, too. Until then, I intend to do my best to keep my inner idiot alive.

I've received frantic calls from frantic store managers, who used the nickname I often go by:

Mall: "Supe, what are you doing this morning?"

Me: "Not too much."

Mall: "We know this is short notice, but can you make it to such-and-such mall, by such-and-such time? We had to take our Santa to the hospital last night, and he won't be making it in today."

Me: "I'll be there."

This is no big deal. Short notice is not a big deal for old guys. Old guys have free time and lots of it. We love it. With a bunch of time on our hands, it is not an inconvenience for us to sit up, suit up, and show up.

This is where something I like to refer to as the Silent Circle of Santas comes into play. It is a simple, unspoken nod or glance between two old guys with white beards, who resemble *him*. When I pull up to a stoplight, alongside a car being driven by a bearded brother, a silent thumbs-up conveys, "Yep, I'm on my way to a gig." I return his nod with a grin. The silent circle will be unbroken.

The light turns green. We go our separate ways. Sometimes, I'm the one upping my thumb, on my way to a gig.

Often, you can see us slowly driving around during a quiet afternoon. Some of us drive long, green Cadillacs with red interior and fuzzy dice dangling from the rearview mirror. Most of us, though, still drive our old, rusted (and *paid for*) pick-up trucks.

> Some may call you Kringle.
> Some may call you Nick.
> No matter what they call you,
> You don't forget his shtick.

Most importantly, remember this: Santa was, Santa is, and Santa always will be bigger than Elvis.

1
Resumé

I remember the exact day it happened. I remember it well. It was on that cloudy morning, when I woke up and looked into the bathroom mirror, that I realized I was starting to resemble Santa Claus. My initial thought was a startled, *Oh, no. I'm starting to resemble Santa Claus!*

Then, my second, unstartled thought was, *Wait a minute. Without a whole lot of effort here, I can actually* be *a Santa Claus. All you really have to do is be fat and funny. I can do that. Being Santa might not be such a bad idea, after all.*

If I just kept my beer belly and let my aging beard grow shaggy and white, I could actually make some extra cash during the month of December as a professional Santa Claus. I had never thought this day would come. But there it was.

Michael Supe Granda

All of this is coming from someone who is *not* a fan of Christmas. Don't get me wrong: I don't suffer severe bouts of holiday depression, like some folks. This particular holiday just doesn't thrill me as much as it seems to thrill others. I much prefer Thanksgiving and Arbor Day.

Though I'm not a big fan of Christmas, I am a big, big fan of Christmas music. Let me clarify. I don't love "Oh, Come All Ye Faithful" or "Little Town of Bethlehem," but I'm a big, big fan of "Run, Run, Rudolph" and "Jingle Bell Rock."

Plus, I love horsing around with little kids. Some of my friends contend that I still am a little kid. But I've always enjoyed little humans, and to get paid for interacting with them is a pleasant side effect of getting old. School teachers, you deserve this same respect—and a raise.

I fondly remember my daughters as sparkling little girls. They've both become wonderful women with their own kids bursting onto the scene. I sigh every time I think of them. I just adore being a silly old grandpa.

There's not much you have to do to become a Santa. The application form is fairly short: Get old. Be jolly. Be gentle. Be cuddly. Be kind. Be funny. Be fat. Grow a beard. Say, "Ho, ho, ho" a lot. That's about it—a job description I could relate to.

I may be a hillbilly, but I'm not a stupid hillbilly. I may only be portraying Santa, but for those little believers, when I put that red suit on, I become *the* Santa. It's a real blast, believe me.

More icing on this cake is that my birthday falls on Christmas Eve. I've been a Christmas baby for every one of my seventy-one birthdays. Every Christmas Eve, right after our evening supper, my father, Bob, would load us kids into our lumbering Ford station wagon for a drive around south St. Louis, to see

Fat & Funny

Christmas lights (wink, wink). While we were gone, my mother, Ellen, would get out all the presents and scatter them under the tree, exactly as Santa would (wink, wink, wink).

Thirty minutes later, we would return home, and my birthday party—I mean, Christmas party—would begin. Grandmas and nephews and neighbors (oh, my!) would come by with bags of gifts and holiday cheer.

When my grandfather, Vic, who worked for Anheuser-Busch, came with cases and cases of Michelob and Budweiser, things began to float. When my crazy aunt Vodka (my godmother and maternal aunt) came by with her infectious laugh, everyone laughed. When my gay uncle Don (my godfather and paternal uncle) came by with his flair and his Fats Domino, Chuck Berry, and Little Richard records, the place erupted. The parties were legendary. My Uncle Don's record collection is where I first acquired my taste for that crazy "BB" (before Beatles) rock 'n' roll.

Year after year, I received only one gift, oftentimes being told, "This is your birthday present *and* your Christmas present." *I know, I know*, I would think. *It's a gyp.* But I didn't really mind, and I still don't. I've never really needed or craved lots of things. I just adored those crazy-ass parties my family threw.

Then, as I grew, I developed a taste for tequila. This sent those parties even further into outer space, sometimes crashing into the moon. The key word is *crashing*.

Many times, the "night before" crashed directly into a head-splitting, Christmas morning. Many years, I spent the morning-after haze in a hungover daze. Many times, I just let December

25 quietly pass on by. Some years, Christmas Day was not a pretty sight. Christmas Eve, though, was always a blast.

I started a rock 'n' roll band in high school. We went nowhere fast, but had an absolute ball getting there. I fell in love with being in a band. To this day, every time I pick up my guitar, I turn into a giant eighth-grader, learning how to play "Get Off My Cloud."

Since then, I've done my fair share of gigs, including 1) a raucous concert in a giant arena, 2) a quiet, acoustic set in a small coffee café, 3) a mellow book signing, and 4) a roomful of anxious children, awaiting Santa. A gig is a gig is a gig. I've had gigs from all of these angles. You will, too. They are all equally important. I completely immerse myself into each performance, musical or otherwise.

Performing has always been a whimsical, fun interest. When I first heard rock-and-roll, I became rock 'n' roll. Everyone who's been bit by this bug, knows the obsession. I obtained tunnel vision and was hooked. I was thrilled to be in a band and still am.

I was also thrilled to audition for and become a cast member in high school plays and productions. I found that the ability to sing and strum the guitar helped in theatrics and vice versa. Plus, I always enjoyed learning new and different songs. I like the proclivity for both sides of this coin, to enhance the other at each gig, no matter the shape or size.

As I went off to college, I helped form another band, which became well known. We made a couple of hit records in the seventies. But we were not a one-hit wonder. No, we had two hits. Unfortunately, they both occurred before the modern age of mega-platinum album sales, leading to mega-platinum rock star wealth.

Fat & Funny

I don't have a lot of money. I'm not a wealthy man. But I am a rich man, because I own my time. Art has allowed me the luxury of living like a complete nut for my entire life, constantly in search of crazy, creative things to do. I realize this. I'm quite thankful. I'm one of the lucky ones, able to make a living as an artist. Oftentimes, "performance is art."

My interests have always been varied. Portraying Santa Claus is just the latest in a long line of old-guy, goofy-guy projects. I take these same approaches with my children's character, Silly Grandpa: come out, act silly, be old, be funny, be lovable, bumble around, laugh a lot, and tickle the kids' fancy and engage their attention.

Rock 'n' roll is a young man's game. Playing Santa is for old guys—jolly old guys who like to hang around, sit around, horse around, and chuckle a bunch. That, I can do. Not every old guy turns into Walter Matthau or Jack Lemmon. Some of us turn into Larry Fine.

I started all this by being a crumpled Santa at several drunken writers' nights and Christmas parties around Nashville, wearing an old, disheveled Santa suit I'd found at a garage sale for a few bucks. Although Billy Bob is a friend of mine, I was not interested in being Bad Santa. I was very interested in being Goofball Santa.

Those evening gigs were a blast. There was no mystery about anything. Everybody knew who was in the suit. They also knew that I—I mean, Santa—never turn down a margarita. I could just mingle among friends, crack a bunch of jokes, get high, and make merry. Most nights, we all ended up on stage, slobbering through our final songs.

Michael Supe Granda

Each year, my beard grew whiter and whiter. Each year, my girth grew wider and wider. I became an older and older fart.

I could tell that my days of being an actual Santa were just around the corner. I could see it in the mirror. I went to a local costume shop and bought a plush, red suit with all the trimmings: black boots; white gloves; red pants; a big, black belt with a big, gold buckle, and some wire-rimmed glasses. I was in business.

The suit is important. It's all you have. This gig does not entail much, folks. When you put on the Santa suit, in earnest, reality melts into myth. When the curtain is down and no one is looking, you can nonchalantly sit around in your suspenders with a cup of coffee and the newspaper. You can be *you*.

But when the jingle bell rings and the curtain flings, the show begins. When this happens, *you* disappear and *he* emerges. He takes over with his mighty, "Ho, ho, ho!" It's his show.

For several years now, I've been a professional Claus and have loved every minute of it. It's a fairly easy gig. I don't have to worry about forgetting lyrics to a song, or being out of tune, while doing it. Santa's musical repertoire spans all the way from "Jingle Bells" to "Jingle Bells." Best of all, I don't even have to bring any kind of guitar, or haul around a lumbering bass amp.

All I have to do is be jolly, comforting, and entertaining to folks, young and old. Plus, most of the time, I don't even have to stand up. It's great. I sit on a big, velvet throne like a velvet couch potato. Believe me—I can couch potato with the best of them.

I just turn into a silly little kid, acting like the silly old man I've become, in and out of the suit. Some folks say I've never grown up. Maybe I haven't. But as *I* have turned into *him*, I've seen many things through my side of his glasses.

I see the holiday spirit.

I see the bah, humbug.

I see the glowing faces and hear the little voices of wonder-filled children.

I see their proud parents.

I see the tears of joy.

I see the unruly kids and their obnoxious, rude, enlarged families.

I see the faces of the children who have recently figured out Santa's shtick, but are in no big hurry to rush over to the aging side.

I see them simply savoring an old man and chuckling at his silly antics.

I see their smiles when I hand them a candy cane. They're still kids.

I also see the scowling people, as they scurry by with absolutely no time, empathy, warmth, or anything for Santa. I find the disdain to be quite sad.

Basically, I see the good, the bad, and the ugly of humanity from behind these specs.

Let me share some of these observations.

On, Dancer.

On, Prancer.

Oh, let's just get on with it.

2
The First Glimpse

Rule 1: The first glimpse is important.

Every time Santa Claus walks into a room, the world stops. Every eye is glued onto the big old goat in the bright, red suit. First impressions and glimpses are all-important. As they say (whoever *they* are), "You don't get a second chance to make a first impression."

This is what you experience every time you suit up and walk

into a room, as Santa. With all those eyes staring at you, you can look directly back at every one of them—all at the same time. In those eyes, I see the stories. I see the joy. I see the pain. I see the ecstatic child. I see the petrified child. I see the calm, understanding teacher. I see the loud, overbearing aunt.

My job is to exclude *none of the above* and have a party with *all of the above.* I also must bring as much goodwill and holiday spirit into the room as I can. After a while, most folks get used to my presence. But when I first start a gig, I lose all identity and sense of self. I fly right out the window, and it's showtime for Santa.

If possible, before anyone arrives, I like to check out the layout of the room. No two rooms are alike. All have different floor plans. I check all the doors. When it's time to enter the room, I've already scouted out the best way to make my splashy entrance. I also know exactly where—and how—to make my strategic exit.

I also check for the bathroom, in case Santa needs one. Old guys are old guys, you know?

Some gigs are expressly for little kids in their school cafeterias. Others are for large companies in their high-rise offices. Some are for adults in rathskellers, while others are for children in malls.

When I walk in, I can immediately spot where I'll be spending most of my time—right alongside the Christmas tree. After all, doesn't everyone want their photo with Santa next to the tree?

All trees, like all rooms, are different. Some trees are tall and hefty. Some are small and spindly. Some aren't even real. Some aren't even green. Some are randomly covered with first-grade ornaments and popcorn strings, while others are adorned with color-coordinated, designer sets from the mall.

Sometimes, there's a soft throne to perch upon.

Sometimes, there's a folding chair.

Sometimes, there's a barstool.

You must learn how to comfortably sit on all of the above.

Still, none hold the sway of a throne. Thrones (seats, in general) cast an important aspect onto Santa. If you've ever wondered why all of the pictures with Santa have him sitting, it is simple. Sitting puts Santa at eye level with the child. A large, red oaf can be intimidating, looming over a kid. A relaxed old man in a chair is much more comforting.

You never know what you're going to get. Every gig is different, though you already know the main theme—*him*. Every gig becomes improv theatre, at its finest. You never know what you're in for when that curtain goes up.

The curtain goes up.

With a loud, guffawing "Ho, ho, ho!" I nonchalantly stroll into the room. But, before I turn my attention to the children, I make it a point to linger about, shake hands, and share laughter with the adults. They usually consist of smiling teachers, proud parents, and family members.

This gives the kids a chance to chill out a little bit and get used to my being in the room. This is a much better approach than smashing right into them with an immediate, jarring onslaught of red.

Oftentimes, when the kids see that I'm being cordial with their moms and their teachers, they figure there's a pretty good chance I'll be cordial with them. Santa's supposed to be a nice guy, isn't he?

Tip 1: Being nice isn't hard—at all.

Tip 2: It takes a lot more time and effort to be a sour jerk (for all of you sour jerks out there). Being nice is much, much easier.

Right before I turn my attention to the kids, I crack a nice joke with the elders. The peal of their laughter makes for a good spot to let loose of their company. Then, I deliver another uproarious "Ho, ho, ho!" into the air.

I can feel the children behind me. I feel their eyes burning holes into the back of my head. I feel their anticipation. I hear them holding their collective breath. I tarry—but not for too long. When I turn around, I hear the collective gasp.

The party starts.

When they approach, one by one, I gather them in my arms to make sure they feel safe, warm and cuddled. This is when I see the young stories in their innocent eyes. I see the funny girl.

I see the bully boy. I see the introvert. I see the extrovert. I look upon all of them in the same way. They all look back at me—I mean, him—in total awe.

I don't worry about the kid who dashes right up and into my arms. No problem there. The repartee becomes insane and immediate. I love the instant lunacy—just add cookies and root beer.

As the gig smooths out and progresses, I like to peer across the room, in search of one of the more reserved kids. I see them at a far table—a safe distance—quietly staring at me. When I wave to them, if they wave back, there's a good possibility I can draw them out of their shell.

Several minutes later, I'll return my gaze to them with another wave, another twinkle, and a hand gesture, indicating they should come and visit. If they still shy away, I just move on to the next kid in line. If they don't shy away, I reanimate the sparkle and clap my hands.

If I see them out of the corner of my eye, inching their way toward me, I just wait them out. There's no need to hurry them. I've got time. We've all got time.

The party continues.

The only way some kids are going to even get near me is in their parents' arms. These kids are very, *very* wary. Some are just shy. Some bury their faces into their mothers' sweaters. Some cry, while others just sob and sniffle. Some suck their thumbs.

Frequently, I will hear a mother say, "Sophia's been so excited to see you, Santa. Haven't you, Sophia? She's been talking about you for days."

Fat & Funny

I'll let out a little chuckle and tickle a foot or belly—nothing to freak them out. Just a little giggle and a big, warm smile.

Another effective icebreaker goes like this. If the guarded little girl is wearing a bright, red dress, I'll start the conversation with an emphatic:

Santa: "Wow! That's a beautiful green dress."

Child: "Santa, that's not green."

Santa (rubbing my eyes in disbelief): "It isn't?"

Child: "No, it's red."

Santa: "Are you sure? It looks green to me."

Child: "*It's red.*"

Santa: "*It's green.*"

(repeat)

Child: "No, it's red."

Santa: "Okay. If you say so, it's red."

When I turn to the other children, they also inform me of the dress's correct color. I just throw my head back, chortle, and act the buffoon. Acting the buffoon never fails to produce laughter.

This banter can continue for as long as needed, until either the bit is over or the ice has melted. Normal conversation and visitation pick right back up.

We all laugh at the same jokes. I join the kids in laughter. If their confused looks are replaced with amused looks, we've cracked another shell.

Boys are a little easier. All you have to do is mention football or monster trucks. That's about the extent of it—short and sweet.

If I am walking around the room, I like to pull up a chair to the crafts table near a bunch of kids and take an interest in their art projects. I use the same shtick, pointing to a picture of a cat and saying, "Wow, that's a cool dog." This starts the same bit and the same *uffoonery-bay* all over again

This is an incredible way to get kids to open up. Art and music are very important and necessary tools for children to become imaginative, well-rounded adults. All children should be vigorously encouraged to express themselves in any creative manner.

Some kids show talent and enthusiasm. Others show no aptitude or interest in art. Still, you treat each masterpiece in the same way. It may only be a picture of a house, some flowers, and the sun. But you treat it as if it's the finest Renoir you've ever laid eyes upon.

When I gasp in amazement, their faces light up. When their faces light up, mine soothes. I encourage each and every one of them to keep singing and making artwork.

I like to single out one of the sillier, friendlier kids and start a running comedy routine. When the rest of the kids see their friend and me joking around and having fun, it's a pretty good indication that it's okay for them to join in the reindeer games.

Sometimes, I'll ask for a piece of paper and a crayon, at which point the kids usually get quiet with anticipation. Their eyes focus on the blank page in front of me, wondering what in the world I'm going to draw.

I'm wondering the same thing. As I scratch my chin and look off into phony space for phony inspiration, I act befuddled. This is also met with sniggles and giggles.

I've learned to draw funny elephants and chickens. Usually, I only draw for thirty seconds. If I have captured the kids' attentions, I can make a longer, drawn-out affair of it. When I ask them which crayon I should use next, I hear a loud chorus of colors.

Pictures of people with ridiculously huge feet and funny hair always get a chuckle. The same goes for pictures of people with funny hats and giant hands playing funny guitars.

After scribbling a silly picture of a dog with six legs or a giraffe with three necks, I stand up and move on to my next focus of attention. I also look to the clock on the wall. Remember, this is still a gig. It's important to remember where your exit is. The time passes.

When Santa's departure is nigh, I slowly begin to drawl, "Well, I guess I'd better get going. I've got toys to make. You boys and girls probably want me to go and start making your toys, don't you?"

This gets them every time. They were glad to see me come. Now, they're glad to see me go.

They want me to get gone and get busy. So, I do just that. I head home and take a nap.

3
Breakfast with Santa

"Breakfast with Santa" is self-explanatory and a wonderful idea. It covers many bases in one fell swoop. These gigs are, obviously, always in some kind of café or restaurant. After all, the marquee does say *breakfast*. Many locales are in malls, with additional shopping in the very near vicinity.

For the price of admission, along with a complimentary photo, a buffet breakfast of bacon and eggs and biscuits and pancakes and syrup and chocolate doughnuts and milk and Froot Loops (kids love Froot Loops) is laid out for the families.

They can bring their entire entourage and share the meal. Tables are pushed together, where folks eat in bunches of six and eight and ten. Kids like to eat breakfast. Everyone likes to eat breakfast. It is quite a money maker for the restaurant.

Grandmas and grandpas, as well as aunts and uncles, all want to spend breakfast time with their little ones. Plus, everyone wants to see their little ones' visits with Santa. The joy is unbound.

Because these gigs are at breakfast and focused on the kids, they are always in the early morning. This is prime time for small children. It's also prime time for seniors. Kids, young and old, share this trait. If you're a Santa, you're automatically a senior, and if you're a little kid, you're already boppin' around by this time of day.

Not only do breakfast gigs provide some pocket cash, they free you up by midmorning, so as to possibly get on to another gig. One particular booking included six appearances to span three weekends.

Because they are such early gigs and I'm not an early riser, by nature, I must pack my Santa suitcase the night before, to make sure *everything* is in it. I also set it right by the door. This way, all I have to do is get up, grab a glass of orange juice, eat a bagel, take a quick shower, and dash out the door.

I reach the ABC Café located in the XYZ Mall by 8:15, and someone shows me to the employee lounge to change. There isn't much going on at this early hour. It is very quiet. Staff is limited, as the place is not really known for breakfast. Normally, most of the staff doesn't come in until 11:00, to prepare for their usual lunch shifts. I'll be long gone by then.

By 8:30, the place begins to fill with families, chowing down and sugaring up. The casual clanging of silverware on plates is widespread. The usual clatter and chatter of children is tempered. Everyone is eating quietly. That will all change soon.

By 8:45, everyone begins to finish up. The clatter resumés. Anticipation mounts. It's showtime.

At 8:50, as the children gather, one of the waitresses reads them a short book. This quiets the kids a bit, soothing them into storyland. I stay hidden from sight, but within earshot, directly behind the kitchen door.

At 9:00, the reader announces that she thinks she hears a special guest nearby. That's my cue. From behind the door and still out of sight, I bellow, "Ho, ho, ho!" into the room. I hear the hush settle through the crowd. Then, I bellow again, jangle my little jingle bell, and slowly stride out the door. Into the fray we go.

By the time I appear, the kids are wiggling in anticipation. When I walk into the room, all eyes are wide and directly upon me.

I clomp around, as I aimlessly amble toward my seat, diverting attention and shaking hands with several of the parents. I like to think this teaches the kids about patience. As I slowly near my spot, I turn my attention to the kids with a loud and enthusiastic, "Now, who wants to come and talk to me?"

As I sit, the restaurant manager funnels the children through a roped queue. One by one, I call them up, jingling all the way. Siblings are led up in pairs and trios. Families approach in bunches.

Fat & Funny

My opening line is always the same, "First things first, kids. Let's all smile for the camera. Then, I want to talk to you." Everyone immediately smiles. Flash bulbs pop. Cameras click. Most of these kids are very cooperative. After all, they've got bellies full of eggs and pancakes.

Then, I just calmly sit and chat. After asking them what they would like for Christmas, I just let them ramble on about whatever it is they want to talk about. When they talk, I laugh. I laugh at every one of their jokes, no matter how simple or disjointed. When I talk, they laugh. I have good jokes. When I chortle, everyone chortles. Everyone needs a good chortle.

This particular restaurant usually seats sixty to seventy people, and this event brings thirty or forty kids up to my perch. Although they all want to see me, none of them want to spend a lot of time with me.

Let me state that another way. The children want to spend time with me, but their families don't. For you see, right outside that front door, there's a whole lot of shoppin' going on and time's a-wastin'.

By this point, everyone is ready to hit the stores. The shop owners, who are just beginning to open their doors for the day, are ready, as well. The kids are literally coaxed off my lap and back into their strollers, which their mothers quickly push out into the mall.

As they jump off my lap and back into the arms of their families, I'm reminded of the brilliance of this whole idea. Right after visiting Santa, the *real world* is right outside that door.

By 9:30, I see the line of kids get shorter and shorter.

By 9:45, their last toy requests are made.

By 9:50, the staff is quickly bussing tables, whisking food away and vacuuming up spilled eggs, napkins, and Froot Loops from the floor. The manager asks me to make one, final stroll around the restaurant to engage the last few stragglers. This is no big deal. I lightly jingle and slowly mingle.

By 10:00, the place is completely empty, and tables are readied for the lunch crowd, which will be arriving soon.

I grab a plate of bacon and eggs and pancakes (no Froot Loops). Then, I head back into the break room, where I quickly take off my suit (so as to not drip maple syrup all over myself) and chow down. I feel as content as those kids I just entertained. I've got a full belly and an entire day ahead of me.

By 10:15, I'm ready to leave, paycheck in envelope in hand in pocket. I can stop by the bank at 10:45 and be home by 11:00. If I'm lucky, I'll have another lunch-time gig. If this is the case, I don't even take off the suit.

Plus, I'm parked right outside the back door. When I arrived earlier, parking wasn't an issue. The lot was completely empty. Now, it is rapidly filling with holiday shoppers. As the mall traffic begins to flood into the *acres of free parking,* I calmly head in the complete opposite direction.

Breakfast with Santa is a cool idea, not only for the kids, but for me too. As droves of noisy shoppers hit the mall, I simply head back out into my quiet life and the quiet day that lay ahead.

4
Your First Gig

As is the case with every performer, there must always be a first gig. Rehearsals are over. Band practices have come and gone. Spring training is melting into the dog days, and the calendar year is fading into the holiday sunset. It's time for the grease paint. It's time to put on your best face, face the crowd, and give it your best shot.

The paycheck, at the end of the gig, is the dangling carrot. But this is your *opening night* and it's time for lights, camera, action. It's also time for you to burst onto the scene, literally. One of Santa's fortes is bursting onto scenes.

When your first gig rolls in, you'll be nervous. You'll be quite nervous and you should be—opening nights are always nerve-racking. That's part of the gig. That's part of the thrill.

There's no business, like show business, my friend. You can't have a long, illustrious string of gigs, without that first one.

Your red suit is ready. Your boots are coal black and your gloves are snow white. Your belly is jelly-jolly. Your "Ho, ho, ho" is razor-sharp. Your beard is aglow. Your game face is on.

You'll remember your first gig for the rest of your tenure. I remember mine, like it was yesterday. It was a quite weird, atypical gig. But there it was. It went a little something like this....

(Rub thy chin. Fade out of thy focus.)

Michael Supe Granda

When the info sheet came in, I learned that I would be Santa from 1:00 p.m. to 4:00 p.m. for a pre-holiday sale at a private residence in a *very* upscale neighborhood, for a *very* rich woman and her *very* rich friends. The carrot was healthy.

Her friends, though, weren't coming to a party. Her friends were hauling in racks, filled with their latest lines of children's fashion. Others were carrying in boxes of their holiday wares (Santa clocks, reindeer coffee mugs and candles, adorned with angels and pine cones).

Because it was my first gig, I made sure I was there in plenty of time. Being early is easy for me; I just don't like to wake up early. *Being* early, though, is no big deal. I've been an early arriver all my life. I've always been one of the first to show up, as well as one of the last to leave. And I know right where this came from—my mother. She was never late for anything. One of my typical conversations with her will illustrate the point.

> Me: "Mama. I've got a gig in town tomorrow night. Would you like to come?"
>
> Mama: "Yes, dear. We're all going. What time do you play?"
>
> Me: "We'll probably start around eight o'clock."
>
> Mama: "Oh, that's nice. Then, I guess we'd better get there at five thirty or six? I want to make sure we get a good table."
>
> Me: "No, Mother. If you just get there a little before eight, I'll make sure you have a nice table."

Mama: "Are you sure?"

Me: "Yes, Mama."

Mama: "Are you sure you're sure?"

Me: "*Yes*, Mama."

Mama: "Okay. See ya then. I love you."

I know she was ready to go at five, and I'm sure she started doing her hair at three thirty. Like her, I have always been terminally early. She was never late for one thing in her entire life. I generally follow in her footsteps, though I have been late for some things. I've been late for airplanes and for breakfast, but I do not like the anxiety that comes with being late for anything. I especially don't like being late for a gig. I abhor it. It is my worst nightmare.

I like to arrive, settle, and spread out, well before the curtain goes up. I would rather sit at an airport terminal gate two hours early than be ten minutes late. Sleeping in and missing breakfast is not so bad. I've done that, quite a few times. But when it comes time for a gig, I am early and already in position.

This is a trait that will benefit you as a professional Santa. Oftentimes, when people hire you, they want to stage you and slot *your* appearance into *their* event. Timelines are important. Being on time is very important.

Remember. Early is good. After all, what would the children say, if Santa was late for Christmas? Plus, this was my first gig.

It was quite early in the season, with weird timing—the Saturday before Thanksgiving. It bothers me when people can't wait until their turkey is digested, to start celebrating Christmas. But the host dictates the time, while the boss writes the check. So, there I was.

I made extra sure I had all my equipment nearby and readied, including my suit, hat, gloves, belt, and smile. I was scheduled to be Santa from one to four, so I arrived a few minutes before 12:47.

It was a beautiful Saturday afternoon with clear blue, suburban skies with highs in the seventies—not your typical Christmas weather. Houses in the neighborhood were expansive and expensive. Air-conditioners blasted away.

When I pulled onto Magnolia Blossom Way, or Southern Rolling Hills Estates, or whatever it was called, I saw that the host's driveway looked like a parking lot, filled with BMWs, SUVs, and small trailers with names like *Mamaw's Little Christmas Shoppe* painted onto the side.

I had time to spare, so I sat in my truck, read the paper, and watched dozens of folks, frantically wheeling in racks of clothing and boxes of knickknacks.

When it came time for this old man to be jolly, I hitched up my pants, straightened my back, locked my truck, weaved down the crowded driveway, and strode into the scene. I didn't carry anything. I dodged numerous carts, chuckling all the way. As Santa, you're required to chuckle—something I really like to do.

When I lumbered in the door and asked for my contact person, I was informed that she was too busy on the chalet's third floor to be involved with the proceedings below. Her personal assistant rushed up with an enthusiastic, "And you must be our Santa?" Duh.

She may have been covered with jewelry and eyelashes. She

was not the sharpest needle on the tree. This first interaction of my Santa career will always be marked by her brilliant observation.

After her initial blurt, she continued, "My name's Chelsea. I'm Ashley's assistant. If you need anything, just find me. Now, come along. We've got you set up in the solarium in back."

From this point on, they will be referred to as Chelsea #1 and Ashley #1.

Chelsea #1 led me through the large parlor, now filled with tables and clothing and shelves of knickknacks. Four trees, fake snow, cookies, and punch were all on display, with cheesy holiday music on the intercom system. Each table was staffed by a woman, who was ready and eager to peddle her latest line of holiday stuff. Their hair was perfect. Their posture was impeccable. Their credit card machines stood at attention with blinking red and green lights.

I was led to a glassed-in back room occupied by a woman (I don't remember her name—let's call her Chelsea #2), who was selling children's clothing and pajamas. She was already sharing the room with another woman (who was probably named Ashley). Ashley #2 displayed her wide array of reindeer pillows, wooden crosses, and decorative plates with Bible verses and manger scenes painted on them.

There, in the corner, I saw my station. It was very quaint, a portrait of Norman Rockwell, with a large, plush chair and an oval rug at my feet. Directly beside all this, stood another perfectly mall-worthy decorated Christmas tree.

This was all nice enough, except for the fact that, by the afternoon, the sun was beating through the big, glass windows of the solarium *big time*. It may have been in the seventies outside, but where I was going to hang out, it had to have been in the nineties. It was hard to sit in that sun wearing my giant, woolen suit. I scooted the chair a little off-kilter to avoid the direct sunlight. Still, I baked.

There, Ashley #2, Chelsea #2, and I sat, awaiting the onrush of holiday shoppers. It was not a good sign, when we were informed that folks might not be showing up until a little later. No one planned on *nobody* showing up.

I could look outside the window and see kids, riding their bikes, kicking around footballs, and enjoying the lovely weather. No one had any desire to go into a massive pre-holiday sale. No one even wanted to go inside, period. It was a warm, autumn day.

Eventually, a few stragglers stopped in. When they did, Chelsea #2 and Ashley #2 snapped into action. So did I—by continuing to just sit there in my chair and watch these two gals get frustrated, that no one was buying, or even looking at their stuff.

To me, all of this was no big deal. All I was doing was—well, nothing. No one was visiting me. I just quietly sat there and watched the clock go around.

Eventually, a handful of well-groomed, well-dressed children walked in with their bejeweled grandmothers. The kids walked up, stood beside me, and smiled for the cameras. Photos were snapped. Then, they quickly ran off, to spend grandma's money. Kids aren't stupid.

By two o'clock, it was obvious that the day's bottom line was *never* going to live up to expectations. A handful of shoppers had come in, but on a balmy day like this, Christmas was the furthest thing from anyone's mind.

As my second hour began, I strolled out into the foyer for

Fat & Funny

some punch and a cookie. It was just as unoccupied as my back room. I could see the disappointment on everyone's faces. They'd gone through a lot of time and effort to haul around their stuff. Some were in grouchy moods. Many weren't filled with holiday cheer.

It was a relief, when Chelsea #1 turned up the air-conditioner, especially for me, sitting back there in my Easy Bake Oven.

Three o'clock brought a few more people, but nowhere near expectations. Ashley #1 emerged from her upstairs boudoir, descending her long staircase with perfect Loretta Young flair. As she flitted from table to table, she was warmly greeted by every vendor. Smiles were forced in her presence.

I'm not sure she could hear the deafening quiet in her house, see all the shoppers not coming, or see all the stuff not selling. It didn't seem to matter to her. She just pranced through. Then, she stopped to smile and watch me on my occupied seat in the sun with my unoccupied lap, not full of children.

Then, she turned on her heel and bolted for the door. Her car awaited, to whisk her off to another, obviously more important, function.

Although some of the vendors were not, I was having a pretty nice time. This was my first gig, and it was as easy as pie. My carrot from Chelsea #1 was going to be organic and healthy. I was jolly and friendly to anyone who wanted to be jolly and friendly. There just weren't many of them. Other than that, I thought my first gig was going along swimmingly.

By 3:05, things got so slow, I was able to take a cat nap in my chair. When I awoke, I could tell absolutely nothing had happened while I dozed.

By 3:15, some of the more impatient vendors began boxing

up and leaving. Although there were no ugly outbursts, I could tell there was some disappointment. Elbows nudged, as they all began to leave.

I continued to just sit and watch Ashley #2 and Chelsea #2 sweating and packaging up their things. I also heard the grandfather clock in the hallway *tick-tock* away. At about 3:30, Ashley #1 walked up with my check. She thanked me and told me that, if I wanted to, I could leave.

While Ashley #2 and Chelsea #2, along with all the rest of the merchants, grumbled under their breath, hauling out boxes of stuff, I whistled a happy tune and wished all a Merry Christmas. I strolled out the door and scampered off, empty handed. This was an easy gig to exit.

Of course, the first thing I did on that warm afternoon, as I headed for my sleigh—I mean, truck—was take off my hat and wipe my sweaty brow. My gloves and coat quickly followed. It was quite a warm day.

Of my ensuing gigs, 99 percent have been merry and wonderful, filled with candy canes, children, and actual holiday spirit. I will admit, this was *not* your typical Santa gig. It just happened to be my first one.

I can't remember my second one, my third one, my twelfth one, or my ninety-fourth one. But I do remember the first one. You'll remember yours, too.

5
Minty Breath

Rule 1: Always maintain minty breath.

Santa is a jolly old man, not a smelly old fart. He may be an old man, but he's not a dirty old man. Santa is for the children. His breath must remain minty and cool. This is why you should always keep a hidden piece of peppermint stick in your pocket. Oftentimes, a bowl of them will be nearby.

When the kids whisper into my ear and I whisper back to them, I don't want to singe their eyebrows with buffalo-wing breath. It's called manners. If they want to continue talking, I'm all ears. If they do, I eagerly become incense, peppermints, the color of time.

You never know where the little tyke's story is going to go. Many begin and end in a big circle, one that usually includes unicorns, cookies, reindeer, their puppy, and their grandma. I just sit and let them ramble. I find this to be quite entertaining. I also know, whenever I want, I can end this whole shooting match with my highly anticipated, "Now, what you would like for Christmas?"

When an entire family descends on you, you more than double, triple, or quadruple your fun. You can immediately see the bossy kids, barging in and taking over. Sometimes, they can become pretty unruly.

You can see the quieter kids drawing back, their eyes like sad saucers. You can tell they probably also have a hard time at home, getting a word in edgewise. Siblings clamor. Five kids, hopped up on M&M's and Mountain Dew can get pretty obnoxious.

When it comes time to take the family portrait, I'll grab a couple of the smaller, meeker kids and set them on my lap. While the big kids might hog the lights, camera, and action, I can make sure the quieter ones get more than their share of my attention.

If they aren't all yelling at the same time, then one by one, I will listen as they talk about their worlds. Often, I'll say, "Who wants to go first?" But before anyone can answer, I quickly point to one of the smaller kids.

If the big'uns insist on hoggin' things, I can turn to them and sternly say, "I'm sorry, but you must wait your turn. That will put you on the nice list." Santa don't take no lip.

Fat & Funny

Then, with a nod of my head, I turn back to the quiet one. We pick up our quiet, little talk where it quietly left off.

When louder kids demand more than their share of my time, I can make sure they get an entire, three and a half seconds of it. I'm Santa Claus, and I can make sure the smaller ones get my full attention and for longer periods of time.

If one of the bossy bunch barges back in, I can invoke another Santa privilege—a stern peer over my glasses, a finger to my lips, and an emphatic, "Shh." Then, it's back to unicorns, reindeers, grandmas, and questions, questions, questions.

"Are you the real Santa Claus?" always gets a chuckle. I respond with an overly emotive, "Ho, ho, ho" (a diversionary tactic) and then quickly change the subject.

"Where are your reindeer?" garners my cagey, "Oh, I had to leave them a few blocks away." Then, I quickly launch into a long and foggy tale of toys at the North Pole (another diversionary tactic).

Many kids are seeing Santa for the first time. I hold lots of infants for their first pictures with Santa. They're a piece of cake. No, really, they are. It's actually like holding a piece of cake.

Just make sure their sleepy faces are exposed and that you don't drop them. That's about it. Snap the photo and hand the kid back—fifteen seconds, at the most. Everyone's happy.

There's a window of three or four years when a child's belief in Santa runs rampant. This is when they're the most fun and adorable. Once, they hit that golden age, when they've figured him out, there's no turning back.

If they don't develop a snotty, "You're not Santa" attitude, most older kids will enjoy hanging around with a goofy old guy and laughing at his stupid jokes.

I only need a handful of jokes. I can use them over and over and over.

1. How do you fix a broken pumpkin? With a pumpkin patch.
2. How do you fix a broken tomato? With tomato paste.
3. How do you fix a broken lemon? With a lemon-aid kit.
4. Why did the cookie go to the doctor? Because he felt crumby.

They work every time.

I started this chapter talking about minty breath. When Santa goes to happy hour, nachos and beer breath are no big deal. We'll get to all that mess in a few pages. But for the most part, when someone wants to draw close and confide in Santa, it's polite to have cool breath. It doesn't matter that you're sweating your ass off in your heavy, red suit. Your breath should remain fresh.

Rule 2: If any children don't want their pictures taken, don't force them.

Most children rush right up and jump into my arms. Others don't. Some of the more freaked-out kids will eventually warm up, but some just won't. Some do not, will not, and never will. Do not force them.

It's not pleasant for anyone, especially Santa. It's not really pleasant for parents. It's not pleasant for the screamer - or the screamees. It's especially not pleasant for all those other little kids standing in line. Your screeching child is putting screechy thoughts into their impressionable heads.

Fat & Funny

We've all seen those funny photos of terrified children, crying on Santa's lap. Yeah, they're funny and all, but not from my perspective. When a child is being brought to the stage against their will, I can instantly read them. Sometimes I'll intervene with a few tricks of the trade I've learned in this short period of time. This is a topic that, just a few years ago, I knew nothing about.

I've stood on stages in front of throngs of people. I've made them stand up, sit down, sing along, clap along, and laugh. There are tricks to that, too. But a degree in child psychology from USC (the University of Santa Claus) gives unique insight to the field. As a matter of fact, we're all outstanding in our field. (Sorry, I couldn't resist the joke.)

One trick I use, is to totally ignore the child, but engage the parents in pleasant conversation. Oftentimes, when children see their parents having a nice time and talking to someone, that someone is probably a nice person.

The chitchat is never more than, "Is your family traveling over the holidays?" or "Have you got all your shopping done?" If the child show signs of thawing, I'll start another batch of banter. Right in the middle of everything, I'll calmly turn to the child and politely ask, "Do you have a Christmas tree?"

If there's any response, I follow up with, "I bet it's beautiful. What's on the top of your tree? Let me guess. Is it an angel, a star, or a pizza?" Bewilderment will quickly be replaced with laughter. Silly works every time.

Simple, friendly gestures can also effectively pull children out of their fear. If they are grasping a small toy, which children often do, ask if you can see it. If they recoil, just abandon the bit. But if they hand you the toy, marvel and gasp at it for a few seconds and then *quickly* hand it right back. Next time you talk to them, you'll find that the ice has been broken.

When the child calms down and settles, I'll give them a little smile, a little tickle, and a big twinkle. Then, a compliment on a snowflake headband helps pave the way.

Then, I turn back to the parents, emphatically instructing them, "Get your cameras ready, right now! *Right now*! We may only have three or four seconds to get this shot, before the screaming starts again."

If the screaming doesn't start, bingo. There's another child who is no longer afraid of Santa Claus.

Another trick is to pretend to be distracted, drowsy, and mere seconds away from nodding off. Not even a squirming child can scream at an old man taking a nap. When the squirming tapers,

I'll stir a bit, yawn, and snap to. If the child seems to be settling, we can move on to the next step, which is the befriending.

If the screaming starts again, there's a pretty good chance you're just not going to get a happy photo. Sorry. Better luck next year. They'll be one year older, and I'll still be sitting here.

When a child is ready to jump right up and into my lap, the fun begins. But before I blatantly ask, "What would you like for Christmas?", a little chat is in order.

There aren't many questions Santa can ask a wide-eyed, three-year-old other than:

> "Are you excited?"
> "Do you have a doggie?"
> "Do you have a kitty?"
> "Do you have a tree?"
> "Have you been good this year?"

In this line of work, nonthreatening is an asset. The kids who aren't intimidated will open up and blossom right before your very eyes. Many will just leap right up into your lap and start blabbing away.

When I assess the spunkiness of a kid or a crowd, I adjust my approach accordingly. Another important Santa asset is the ability to think quick on your feet – or, your lap.

Some kids aren't so sure about Santa, wanting to keep him at arm's length. That's fine. They're friendly enough; they just don't want anything to do with all the cuddling and hugging. No problem there, little one.

For many of the boys, a simple, "Hey, dude. Gimme five" should suffice. For the girls, a compliment on their shiny shoes should work.

Some kids are real hams. Some just aren't. I love kids, but I don't want to traumatize a child just for the sake of a stupid picture. Out-of-control, screeching children are not fun.

Rule of thumb: Play it by ear.

Rule 3: Drunks are oftentimes worse than the kids.

Occasionally, you will get two challenges at the same time. Tipsy adults will bring their sugared-up kids to see Santa. Their un-minty breath is often accompanied by the sweet stench of nicotine. There's nothing sadder than to see a sweet, little girl with the aroma of secondhand cigarette smoke in her hair.

Act accordingly. But whatever you do, don't bring up the subject of liquor. Everyone's listening. Everyone has a cell phone with a camera. Children can't file lawsuits, but drunks can. Just sit there, smile, talk to the little ones, and bid everyone a fond, quick adieu.

Ninety-eight times out of a hundred, things will be cool. If a situation does get a little uncomfortable, it's usually a rude child emulating a rude parent. It's not a pretty sight. At these moments, I exercise Santa's right to not converse a whole lot, take the damn picture, and move on to the next visitors, as fast as he can.

Still, you must not be rude. You're still Santa. You're still getting paid. Many times, all I can do is sigh at the thought of what their home lives must be like.

Who wants their picture taken with Santa? Lots of people. They come in two categories: 1) happy, nicely dressed people celebrating the holidays, and 2) dour, slovenly people who don't

Fat & Funny

crack a smile and want to tell you all about their problems. They can be a little hairy, too.

There is a glut of selfies. You will appear in two million of them. Most of the shots are pleasant and quick. Take every one asked of you. Taking a picture is one of the main reasons you're getting paid. It's just part of the gig. You shouldn't have a problem with this.

No one is going to notice you in the shot, anyway. Nobody will be looking at you. Their focus is going to be on the other folks in the photo.

There you have it. Three rules I just made up, out of thin air. There'll be more—if they come to mind. My mind, though, isn't what it once was.

Until then, remember to keep your breath minty, try to make the little kids smile, and try to ignore the horrible adults.

Rule 4: TBD

6
Pretty Flowers

The morning was a bit slow. An uneven stream of folks had stopped by, but it was nothing overwhelming. Santa hadn't even broken a sweat. All in all, it was quite a pleasant morning. I was having a nice time just being an old guy, sitting on the throne.

When I sit as Santa, I have a bird's-eye view of the entire proximity. I see everything—jolly children, scowling adults, young couples, new parents cradling their first infant, large families of nieces and nephews and uncles, oh, my.

I saw her silhouette at the top of the hallway. She walked and skipped down into the atrium, where I sat. She lit up the entire place. Barely able to contain herself, her uncontrollable fits of jumping and clapping and clasping her hands, made me smile.

When she caught her first glimpse of me, she was transfixed.

Then, she started waving her arms in complete ecstasy, her pigtails bouncing at her sides. When we made eye contact, she twinkled. I twinkled back. I knew her visit was going to be wonderful. I couldn't wait. She and her mother got in line.

Although it was relatively quiet, several small groups stood before them. Sometimes, the line can wind all the way around the room. Other times, there are lulls in the action. During the lulls, I just basically sit there, write lyrics in my head, and look around.

If I see a traffic jam of people forming, I've learned how to manipulate the crowd. More importantly, I've learned how to dissipate them. I call forth the biggest group, gather them around, ask a couple simple questions, snap their picture, and quickly help them vacate the premises.

This not only alleviates congestion; it frees up space for others. When I see someone special come along, I can also nonchalantly and effortlessly squeeze them in, at the front of the line.

She beamed at the edge of the crowd, in anticipation. She danced at her mother's feet, shining coast to coast, like a starry, starry night.

All dressed up, she was going to see Santa Claus. She was on top of the world—and I don't mean the North Pole top of the world. She sparkled like the North Star.

Her spangled green dress was adorned with elves across the front. Her Christmas socks matched the bows in her hair. At her side, she carried a clear plastic, reindeer purse, filled with whatever five-year-old girls carry in their clear plastic, reindeer purses. I couldn't wait to visit with her.

I turned to greet the next family in line—a large gaggle of

large people, dressed in their finest holiday overalls and their nicest baseball hats. I could tell the only reason these grumbling kids were there, was at their mother's insistence on their photo with Santa.

I call these Smile Rusty situations. I can spot a Smile Rusty coming from a mile away. I hear "Damn it. Smile, Rusty" from over my shoulder. Usually, the yeller isn't wearing a smile, either. So, there you go.

But when I see excited kids, I feel an obligation to get to them and get to them quickly. They're excited. They deserve to get to me quickly. I can make that happen, even if adults are next in line.

She politely waited by her mother's side, as her father walked up from the parking lot. It was almost time for the little one to meet the big one. She gave me another sheepish wave and quietly stood in the line, which wasn't too long. I could tell she would be up to see me, shortly. I waved back.

An infant was placed into my arms. This always makes me a bit uneasy. Thankfully, most of these little bundles are just that—actual bundles. I hold the bundle up to the camera and smile. *Click*. I hand the baby back, and we're done. The whole ordeal only takes a few seconds.

Next, a young couple in love sidled onto the couch, on either side of me. They were very pleasant to visit with and very much in love. She flashed her newly acquired diamond ring, which was petite and fit her finger well. I like rings, like this. I like people, like this.

I could tell *he* had saved his wages to buy *her* that ring. I could also tell she was thrilled and proud to wear her tender gem (no matter, how modest). I could see that the little stone was filled with more love and affection than most gaudy, obnoxious bling rings are. Her ring was very *ungaudy* and very *unblingy*. I liked it.

After a warm chat, they turned to the camera. We all smiled, and they were gone in seconds. Young couples just adore having their pictures taken with Santa. Years from now, they'll be able to look back on their good ol' days, and I'm honored to be part of them.

Only one more small family in line. As I let each child ramble, I glanced over at the little sparkler, still patiently and politely waiting at the head of the line. Her mother was busy combing her hair and straightening her dress.

From her reindeer purse, she grabbed her Santa list. I scooted up to the edge of my seat. *Bombs away,* I thought. *Here she comes.*

When it was her turn, she sprinted right up to my couch and rushed right into my arms. I was prepared. You should always be prepared. I saw her coming. I softly and easily caught her. I guffawed as she dove and buried her face into my coat.

I can tell when an excited child is about to come in for a crash landing. I know how to easily catch them, nestle them, and give them big, fuzzy hugs.

When I motioned for her to sit next to me, she jumped right up. We both settled back into the arms of the couch. I crossed my legs and gently held her hand. We started to talk. I wanted this visit to last.

I glanced back at the next folks in line. It was a married couple in matching leather Dallas Cowboy jackets. They were just going to have to wait. I was talking to Shirley Temple.

I started with my standard questions. They elicited standard answers. By this point, I can usually tell if a child is going to become chatty, or not. I knew from her polite, articulate answers that she was a dynamo, just waiting to happen somewhere. When she glanced up at me, her eyes were as big as blue tubas.

I softened my gaze, to let her know that she was in safe hands. Then, she just exploded, veering off into subjects as wide, whimsical, and sweet as could be.

I didn't have to say a word. I just sat there and listened, completely amused. I wasn't the only one captured by her. As she rambled, I could see a crowd gathering around us, hanging on her every word. There were quite a few words. There were quite a few people. Everyone was just as enthralled as I was.

She showed me her list. There wasn't much on it. Her note, though, was artistic and spectacular. With crayons and stickers and glitter (oh my), I started to read under my breath.

When I finally got around to asking her name, she scrunched her shoulders, smiled, and spouted, "Daisy." The peanut gallery went wild.

When I asked what she wanted me to bring her for Christmas, she shouted, "Flowers!" The peanut gallery went wilder.

My heart melted into a pool of egg nog. The enrapt crowd audibly *aww*ed. I bit my lip. It was all I could do, to not tear up. On occasion, this does happen.

At times, like this, little girls, like this, remind me of my own sweet, lovely daughters when they were small girls. They've both become sweet, lovely women. But, in their eyes, I still enjoy seeing sweet, little girls.

When I asked Daisy if she wanted any particular kind of flowers, she scrunched her nose and exclaimed, "Pretty flowers!" The peanut gallery came unshelled. Everyone within earshot exploded with laughter and applause. I rolled my head back and ho-ho-howled. She howled, too, as she bounced up and down.

Fat & Funny

With a hug and an enthusiastic, "I love you, Santa Claus," she bounded off the couch and skipped back to her mother's side. I was genuinely touched.

When the next couple sat down beside me, smelling of football and tobacco, I did my best to take their picture and move them on along. By this time, the length of my line was growing. When this happens, individual visits get shorter.

While I started chatting with the next folks, I could see Daisy off to the side, perturbed about something. As she cried and pleaded with her mother, I could see that she still had her wish list in her hand. She had gotten so excited, she had forgotten to leave it with me.

I immediately recognized what was happening. I made the next group of kids wait and waved Daisy back up. She bolted like lightning and handed me her list.

I thanked her again. She hugged me again. Then, with another "Bye. I love you, Santa Claus," she skipped off down the hall. I kept my eye on her, as she strolled, hand in hand with her dad.

Thirty feet down the hall, she turned and looked over her shoulder. I wasn't about to let her down. I was there to return her one last glance.

We smiled. We waved. I never saw her again.

Pretty flowers for Santa, indeed.

7
Santa Meter

Rule 6: Check the Santa meter before your appearance.

Every Santa gig is different. You can count on them to be as unpredictable and as crazy as a rock 'n' roll gig. Three dozen sugared-up five-year-olds can raise quite a ruckus. They can give any rock band a run for its money, in intensity *and* volume.

The piercing squeal of a screaming child can easily out-shrill the feedback of a slashing guitarist. On the other side of this coin, the slobberings of a drunken grown-up can easily match the blubbering of a thick-tongued singer.

When you're hired to be Santa, the first thing you should do is get the particulars (e.g., Where? When? Until when?). The next thing I do is ask my agent for a reading on the Santa meter. Oftentimes, this meter will be your *most* important bit of knowledge. Yes, the Santa meter is a good barometer. No, the Santa meter is not on the metric system.

'ONE' on the meter is a traditional Santa. These gigs are as safe as milk and a piece of pie. If you wish, you can call them mall gigs. You just quietly sit there, hand out a few candy canes, and listen to the little children, who are in complete awe of your big, white beard and your bright, red suit.

These gigs usually take place in the morning, when kids are at their most playful. I might not be at my most playful at that time of the morning. But as I just mentioned, all I have to do is sit there and smile at the camera.

'TEN' on the meter is your rock 'n' roll Santa gig. Sometimes, these 'TEN' gigs can actually get turned up to "ELEVEN". They are also a lot of fun. Children are definitely not a part of these equations. The galas are gaudy, and Santa is usually invited to partake of whatever holiday spirit the revelers are dishing.

And, as we all know, Santa loves to drink tequila and sing into the night. Hmm. That's funny. Those are the same things I like to do. Yep, Santa and I both love happy hour.

Settings between 'ONE' and 'TEN' are just variations on a theme. If you're mingling with total strangers, just remember to mind your p's and q's, watch your tongue and don't step on any toes. If you're mingling with friends, go ahead and toe step.

Both 'ONE' and 'TEN' are equally fun. The distinction, though, between Kris Kringle and Billy Bob should be determined in advance.

'TWO' on the dial is when the children convene during school hours in their cafeteria. These are usually strict, regimented gigs under the watchful eyes of teachers. Sometimes, I'm hired to just walk in, wave to the kids, hang around for thirty minutes, "ho, ho, ho" a few times, shake some hands, slap some backs, blow a few kisses, hug some children, wave good-bye, and exit stage left.

'THREE' is when the children convene for their annual Christmas parties. Most of these parties take place on weekends. They're often held in quainter facilities. The less-frenetic crowds are smaller and usually contain a closer-knit group of friends. These gigs may be tinier, but they're no less festive. They're also quite fun for me. With some planning, I can schedule several of these "gigettes" into the same day, hopping around town, from one party to another.

'FOUR' is when I'm invited into someone's home for a private appearance at an extended family affair. Usually, a rich uncle or a silly grandpa wants to pony up part of his Social Security check for some 'live' entertainment for his grandkids. As the youngsters clamor inside, I stand in the quiet shadows of the garage, quietly chatting with some of the grown-ups. Our Dick Tracy watches are synchronized. So is our Santa script.

Inside, I can hear the kids bouncing off the walls. Usually, they're still young enough to believe in Santa and have been foaming at the mouth for a month to see him.

When the adults nonchalantly reenter the party, the fun begins. I tell them to just stroll back in, grab a glass of wine, and wait a few minutes for the show. I sit on the dark porch for a bit. Then I begin to make a ruckus at the front window.

Sometimes, I'm handed a pillowcase, filled with presents. I make sure, ahead of time, that I have the exact number (don't want any child to not receive a gift) and that each has a name tag (don't want Missy to open a football helmet or Mikey to open a dollhouse).

Everyone screams when I ring the doorbell.

I walk in, hug the onrushing kids, and head to the den. Here, I see the same grown-ups I was just talking to, out in the dark. Now, awash in the glow of Christmas lights, their beaming faces reflect the euphoria in their children's eyes.

I do not just walk in and start handing out presents. I gather all the kids at my feet and begin a relaxed, soothing conversation with them. I see their eyes, transfixed on my bulging pillowcase. It quietly sits on the floor, right beside me.

Fat & Funny

The anticipation is wonderful, as I deliver their lesson in patience. I don't leave the kids hanging on for too long, though. Their replies are cordial and can get quite esoteric. They are also very energetic. They can go on and on and on, as long as they want. I'm always amused—with a capital *muse*.

I instruct the parents to get out their cameras and be ready at the drop of a hat. When the flashes begin to go off, I know how to direct each child's focus toward Grandma's lens.

After a slight cooling off period, I begin to fiddle with the sack of toys. But instead of just tossing them around and yelling, "Here you go!" I demand that no one opens a gift, until everybody has one. This is a lesson in manners, as well as patience.

I get them all dispensed, count down from five, four, three-three-three-three-three, two, one, and step back from the shredding. When the fray begins, my work is pretty much over. The kids dive in headfirst. They are frantic, loud, and in seventh heaven.

The next item on the agenda is my impending exit. After a while, as the kids begin to disperse and head back into their own little worlds, they pretty much ignore me. The party's over—at least, my part. I loudly proclaim that I've got to get back to the North Pole and bid everyone a fond adieu.

After I leave, their party will continue into the evening. I shake everybody's hand, one of which has a Christmas card with coins in it. Santa deposits the card into his boot and begins a slow, emotive trek toward the door.

When I walk outside, I can still hear and feel the warmth of the family behind me. As their lights continue to flicker, I walk into the dark, climb into the quiet of my truck, and head off into the night.

These gigs are over in about thirty minutes. They end early, too. Sometimes, when they end, it's still happy hour. Most times, my faithful elves have a cold beer waiting for me, in my sleigh.

Back to the Santa meter. 'FIVE' is the sophisticated, evening, cocktail soiree or office party, complete with champagne fountains and bubble machines.

A reading of 'SIX' means the alcohol is beginning to take effect.

'SEVEN' registers high on the decibel reader. Everyone has just gotten off work and has yet to change clothes. Ties may loosen. Hair may fall. Still, the party is as starchy as a tuber. The longer the party lasts, the more it lets loose. But, not much. These folks know how to get off to a slow start.

Everyone's in a good mood. It's Christmas. Everybody's nice. Everybody's flirty. Everybody's playing grab ass. I can see it all around me; I just pretend not to. I say nothing. It's their office party, for Pete's sake. They can do whatever they want.

As the party continues, Santa does his little dance and joins in. They may have set up a chair by the tree. Most times, though, I just hang out with the people, blend into the group, make merry, do a little jig to a couple songs, and take a few photos with the boss and his staff.

Guys just want to hang out and crack dirty jokes with Santa Dude, while clutching cans of beer. Santa Dude photos are very quickly snapped. There is no staging. There is no repositioning. There are no second takes. Handshakes are replaced with fist bumps. Fist bumps appear more often, with the introduction of Bocephus hats.

Women want their picture taken with Santa, too. They would rather sit demurely on his lap. I have no problem with this. We sit.

Some women are fresh and breezy. Others are stale and aromatic.

Some are funny and bubbly. Others are lonely and flirty.

Some are fresh from the farm. Others are fresh from the condo.

Some just climbed down off their tractors. Others just climbed out of their surgeon husband's helicopter.

Some jangle their jewelry, when they walk. Others still have mud on their boots.

Some don their gay apparel. Others don their best sleeveless T-shirts.

Some smell like puppies and flowers. Others smell like beer and cigarettes.

I just sit there, treat them all the same (like I do with the children), and compliment them on their perfume, no matter how much they've slathered on.

At some point during the party, the boss usually wants to "address his people." This is a good time for Santa to quietly shuffle out of the spotlight and quickly find the back of the room. It's break time for me.

Some bosses want to fulfill their stand-up comedian fantasies, so they ramble on and on. As far as I'm concerned, this is not a problem. They're paying the bill. I'm watching the clock. They can bullshit as long as they want. While everyone's attention is focused on them, I've got time to visit the restroom.

If the bosses are dolts, their entire oration can take less than twelve seconds. Once again, they're paying the bills. I just hike up my belt and reenter the fray.

Some parties last from happy hour to happy hour-thirty. These are usually low-key. Everyone wants to socialize a bit, mingle, then move on. Many will attend other functions. This is also fine with me. When everyone leaves, I just head to the house. Other parties may last longer. I don't mind. I get paid, accordingly.

If the party is from five thirty to six thirty, no one can really get too hammered, in that short amount of time. If the party is from five thirty to eight thirty, there's plenty of time for folks to get that hammered. And if the party is from nine thirty to eleven thirty, you can count on an entire tool belt of hammers.

However, if it's an office luncheon from ten to eleven in the morning, it'll usually be a nice, polite affair that is quite enjoyable. These gigs resemble my Silly Grandpa gigs, which are generally around this same time of the day. Thankfully, no one wants to get hammered at eleven in the morning.

On the Santa meter, 'EIGHT' and 'NINE' are just variations on 'FIVE', depending on how quickly the party flows from first cocktail to many cocktails. At some parties, people invite Santa to imbibe with a drink and some food. I usually pass on the drink, though I may ask for a quick snort of tequila (beer makes me pee). I do not, though, pass on a plate of food. After all, I must keep up my fine physique.

Level 'TEN' is the highest the Santa meter goes. Sometimes, 'TEN' devolves into a debacle, of which you want no part. When I sense an impending train wreck, I ask for my fee before I even

Fat & Funny

start. You don't want to deal with a drunken host at the end of the party, who can't find their keys, their cigarettes, or, more importantly, their checkbook.

The moral of this story is that you should check the Santa meter before you turn into Santa. You'll thank me in the morning.

8
Small-Town Friday Night

not every Santa gig is a glamorous one. Most are held in pleasant malls, plush stores, and the cozy homes of cozy people, who can afford a few extra bucks to hire a real Santa with a real beard. Some gigs just aren't as glitzy.

One gig was in a typical small town, in the heart of the country. When I looked up its location, I learned that it would take a couple hours of driving to get there. The gig's early start got me out of my house in plenty of time, to be Santa on time.

Anytown, Tennessee, is a rural community of a couple thousand people, located along the Tennessee and Kentucky border. It is easy to tell that, in order for these folks to get to some big-city culture, it would take a concerted effort and several hours of driving.

The particulars of the gig are as follows: "2016 Christmas Festival of Lights," featuring pictures with Santa from 5:00 to 9:00 p.m. All of this was fine and dandy, except for the fact that I would be in an outdoor setting. Anything outdoors in December is always a roll of the dice, even in the mid-South. Sometimes, it can be relatively comfortable. Other times, it can be downright frigid. Then, there's always the chance of precipitation. It's a gamble. Seven, come eleven.

When I arrived, it was happy hour on a Friday, and the small town was semi-bustling. Although there wasn't an actual town square, the five-block stretch of Main Street/main drag sufficed. The street was blocked off and filled with women, setting up booths and filling them with home-made pastries, candles, jellies, and knitted things for holiday shoppers.

Christmas music wafted up and down the street. This was not a humongous undertaking. Still, it felt very homey and comfy. When I arrived at 4:40, the sun was still up and the outdoor air was brisk and refreshing. Anytown was alive with a quaint, old-fashioned spirit.

If you're asking yourself, why these folks wouldn't just find a local guy with a white beard to be Santa, there are a couple reasons. One of the main ones is, though there are many local men with big, white beards, who could easily pass as Santa, they're still a friend of a friend of a family friend. He wouldn't be able to fool the children. These men might be willing to don the big red suit, but they'd still be Bob the plumber or Clyde the propane guy. No mystique there.

Michael Supe Granda

By hiring an outsider, they get someone new, from somewhere different. When people encounter Santa, there needs to be a sense of mystery shrouding him, wherever he goes (especially for the kids). As a seasoned *him*, I know how to pace proceedings and handle situations that may arise. When in doubt, hire a professional. When your plumbing backs up, call Bob.

I was shown into the city hall, where I was led into a large room that looked like it had been used as a banquet hall/meeting room for the other 364 days of the year. There, I dressed and transformed under florescent lights, organization banners, American flags, and photos of the city council.

When five o'clock rolled around, I looked out the window and across the street. My throne awaited. I would like to say something spectacular and descriptive about the scene, but it was just a short distance across an empty parking lot, where I was to sit for the next four hours.

When showtime came, I opened the front door and bellowed, "Ho, ho, ho!" Always bellow, "Ho, ho, ho!" when you open any door. Then, I stomped down the steps of the place, plodded across the parking lot, and settled onto my perch, warmly nestled against the brick wall of the local hardware store.

A professional photographer set up twelve feet in front of me. Her lights and lamps were a source of warmth—but not much of one. As I sat down, a line of kids gathered in awe of the big, red presence. When an advertisement around this place says, "Pictures with Santa at 5:00," it means just that. By 5:01, the games had begun.

Unlike many of my other gigs, where the children brush their hair and don their finest Christmas apparel, these kids were still clad in the thermal boots and hats they had worn around the farm all day.

This would be their only chance to talk to Santa, for the year. As they approached, I tried to be my usual, friendly, affable self. Still, I sensed apprehensions—the same apprehensions they had, when they met strangers in their daily lives.

When they walked up, many smelled like the tobacco their folks had been smoking in the cabs of their trucks, on their way into town. How depressing it is, to see a pretty little girl with a bow in her hair, reeking of secondhand cigarette smoke.

The families were larger in size than I normally see. Usually, I'm faced with families of two or three. That's easy for the photo—one child on each side. But here, I faced families of five and six kids, requiring actual choreography. I left this to the photographer. She was a local. She knew all these folks. They liked her. She arranged them around me, for each shot. I just sat there.

When I looked out, through the lights, I could see the rest of each child's family (moms, dads, aunts, uncles, grandmas, and grandpas), also clad in every shade of brown and khaki in the rainbow. Some smelled of alcohol. Others sported chewing tobacco in the corners of their mouths. I was a long way from the cozy corner of the cozy mall.

I could also tell I was a long way from the cozy mall, when many of the kids, instead of asking for iPads and dollhouses, asked for shotguns and four-wheelers. All I did was smile, hand out high-fives, and send them on their merry ways.

Before I did, though, there was the task of taking the picture. Some will easily smile. Some won't. In fact, some never do warm up. Some can't. I just hit my autopilot switch, and let things happen.

Usually, I don't notice and can't tell whether the kid is smiling, because I'm looking at the camera with a smile of my own. But I know the child *isn't* smiling, when I hear, "Damn it, Jeff. Smile!" blurted from the dark. When a situation gets sticky or awkward, I use my Rapid Santa Pass to take a quick photo, wish everyone a Merry Christmas, and quickly send them back into the chilly evening.

Family after family stopped by. Most were pleasant, seeming to enjoy the old guy in the red suit. They laughed at his silly antics and jokes. Others weren't as humored or humorous. Others were downright droll and grumpy. A good indication was, when their baseball hat informed folks of their intention to make America great again.

A large tractor, pulling a flatbed trailer, ambled by every fifteen minutes. Filled with bales of hay, an actual hayride stopped in the parking lot near my spot. I could see families quickly disembark and slowly meander toward me.

By six o'clock, most of the townsfolk, who wanted to see Santa, had seen Santa. By six thirty, the line had dissipated. The occasional family stopped by. By seven o'clock, after a couple hours, the focus of the festival shifted downtown, to a very quaint city park. A local bluegrass band played old standards and Christmas carols. Mark Twain is alive and well.

By seven thirty, the sun had gone down. So had the temperature. It is times like this, that I'm thankful to be wearing a warm hat, a thick suit, and big boots. The photographer's husband, also clad in camo, handed me a couple of hand warmers, which he used when turkey hunting. They worked very well. I put them inside my gloves and shook his hand.

Directly across the street sat the tallest building in town—the courthouse. It was all dressed up for the holidays, with lights and wreaths and a manger scene at the foot of its spire. A large, well-lit clock could easily be seen from anywhere in town, including my parking lot perch. All I had to do was look up to see what time it was. Clocks move slowly in this part of the country.

At eight o'clock, the tree-lighting ceremony began. This completely emptied my area, which was no big deal to me. I strolled around the corner of the hardware store and looked up the block. As I listened to the mayor's countdown, I was counting down the minutes, until I would be finished. Five, four, three, two, one—the tree illuminated. The bluegrass band launched into rousing versions of "Rocky Top" and "Jingle Bells," followed by a soothing version of "We Wish You a Merry Christmas."

By eight fifteen, I had turned around and gone back to my position. The hayrides had stopped, as had all of the festivities around my wall of the hardware store. Still, I sat in the quiet parking lot, conversing with the photographer and a handful of her friends. She was just as eager for the night to be over as I was. We both eyed the clock tower.

At eight twenty, the festival's coordinator stopped by, to see how we were doing. When she saw that there was absolutely no action, or any prospect of action, she told us to just shut it down and handed us our checks. Pleasantries went around, for a job well done. While the photographer was dismantling her lights and camera, I gathered my things and headed for the car. It was a nice evening. It didn't rain or snow.

Although most of these folks would soon be as snug as a bug

in their homes, I still had a two-hour drive back to Nashville. This wasn't a big deal. I've been driving home from late gigs for over fifty years. Two hours is nothing.

The drive out of Anytown was a quick one. The lights of the city faded in mere minutes, Highway XYZ took over, and the dark of night settled in. Thoughts of the evening's gig quickly turned to thoughts of tomorrow morning's gig—in a comfy, cozy Nashville mall.

9
Lists

One of the many traditions around Christmas, along with trees and lights and eggnog and fruitcake, is the making of lists. They're on refrigerators in kitchens, all over the world. They're on the backs of envelopes. They're on torn pieces of cardboard. Some are written onto palms of hands.

Lists are taken into stores and malls, as people shop for holiday gifts. They are taken into grocery stores, as families prepare for holiday feasts.

Who hasn't done their shopping with a list in their hand? They are absolutely essential. For people my age, our memories are so shabby, we can't go near any store at any time without a list.

Plus, what child hasn't lovingly and painstakingly spent their day writing out a Christmas list? We all know, thoughts of Santa are smack-dab in the middle of every one of them.

They're everywhere. The list goes on and on.

Plus, in Santa lore, we have the addition of the nice list and the naughty list. The two walk hand in hand. Obviously, the nice list is for the nice kids. The naughty list is just an idle threat, to help kids hop back over the fence to the nice side.

For me, as Santa, they're also a bunch of bunk. I've never kept a list of who is naughty and who is nice, and I've never checked it twice. Hell, I haven't even checked it once.

Of course, all parents know there is no way their precious children are on any kind of naughty list (wink, wink). The naughty list is just a nice way to get kids to be nice. If not, parents can invoke, "Or, there'll be no Christmas visit from you-know-who" (wink, wink, wink).

Of course, when you ask three-year-olds if they've been nice, 999,999 times out a million, their answer will be a quick and emphatic *yes*. What child, in their right mind, is going to tell Santa Claus they haven't been good?

Adults, on the other hand, will willingly admit to naughtiness. When adults confide that they've been really bad this year, the jokes begin to write themselves. The laughing is instantaneous. Young or old, it doesn't really matter. The jokes are just a little funnier when there's a little naughty in the mix.

I have a complete and separate set of comebacks, jokes, banter, and shtick for each category. Talking to children about the nice list is one thing. Talking to adults about the naughty list is a lot more fun.

Then, you have the most important of all—each child's personal list to me. I see it in their hands, as they patiently wait in line. They may have come to see me, but I also see them. Many times, from where I sit, I spot them before they spot me.

They clutch those little lists in their little fists, as if they were the most important things in their little worlds and made of gold. That is because they *are* the most important things in their little worlds—and they *are* made of gold. This gift-getting thing only comes around once a year, and this is their time to shine. This is their time to tell me what they want for Christmas. As Santa, I'm not going to rain on any kid's parade.

When children walk up, I know they're eager to dive right into

Fat & Funny

lists and toys and presents and such. I ask a few easy questions and waste a little time. A little anticipation never hurt anyone. That's why I keep my opening salvos rapid-fire, followed by a handful of spaced-out, old-guy sighs.

Then, I will finally ask them what they've got in their hands. Once again, 999,999 times out of a million, the list comes my way in $1/999,999^{th}$ of a second. Some are nicely written on holiday stationery with glitter, tidy doodles, and polite penmanship. Others are scribbled across scraps of paper and cardboard with crayons, pencils, sticks, or whatever else the kid could find.

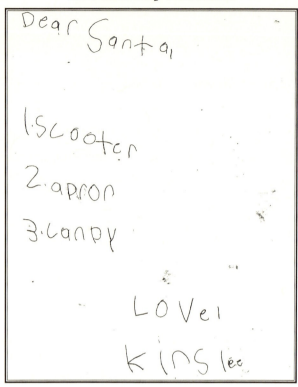

Some are very legible. I enjoy reading them. I draw the kids near as we quietly and slowly go over the list. One by one, each item is discussed. When I feel the kids begin to relax, I know they've started enjoying *us* time.

Even if I've never heard of some of the newer toys, I nod my head as if I have. "Oh, yeah. Sure," is a usual response, followed by "Yes, I'm familiar with that." It works every time.

Some lists are total chaos and completely illegible. Some resemble hieroglyphs more than calligraphy. Even if I can't make out one single word, I pretend that I can. Oftentimes, I ask children to do the actual reading, along with most of the talking.

Some lists are softly handed over in nice, aromatic envelopes. Some lists are unfolded from linty pockets. Some lists are artwork, and some lists arrive on sticky, wadded-up Christmas paper. Each one is just as cool and wonderful as the next—a beautiful expression from an innocent mind.

I look forward to each one, no matter the shape, size, or legibility. I know each note has been carefully and repeatedly mulled over. I also know it was a *very* important part of that child's day. I handle each one, as if it's the most important thing I've seen all morning. That's because, it *is* the most important thing I've seen all morning.

As I'm having my initial chat with the children, I glance up at the parents. This way, I can gauge how to approach the actual reading of the list. If the parent has helped the child and already knows what's on the list, I can just immediately turn back and proceed with the kid. We snuggle and begin to read. If the child is the quieter type, our visits are pleasant, light-hearted, and free of screeching cousins. If the child is boisterous, all I have to do is sit there and listen, like a couch potato. Piece of cake in either situation.

If their penmanship is impossible to decipher, I'll ask them to read their list to me. As they rattle off each toy, I respond to each with consenting nods, "Yes, yes, yes," and "Ho, ho, ho."

Of course, I know what Legos are. I know what skateboards are. I know about Barbie playhouses and football helmets. I know what an Easy-Bake Oven is. But if children mention a toy that I'm not that familiar with, I may say, "Hmm. Nice. Tell me a little more about it." Sorry, folks. I just don't know what some of them are. If it has "2000" or "Furious" in its name, I'm pretty much out of the loop. I know. I know. I'm supposed to know all about every toy made by my elves. Blah, blah, blah. I've gotten good at faking it. You should develop this ability, too.

Fat & Funny

Often, their sheer excitement sends them into ecstatic, detailed descriptions of the toy. It's very cool and very entertaining. If you have four sugared-up five-year-olds telling you what they want at the same time, it can get fast and 2000 in a hurry.

If children are more reserved and don't really want the whole world to know what's on their list, it's not my job to broadcast that info. This is a tender moment of confidentiality between child and Santa. I'm not about to break that trust.

Also, don't rush right through any list. Remember, this is a gig. You're still on the clock. Dragging your feet is a viable, valuable option. Lollygagging through a long, drawn-out wish list is a very effective waste of time (like an extended, drunken guitar solo).

I may ask a question or two, just to get the child to open up and converse more. Then, we turn right back to the list and pick up where we left off.

If I see a parent leaning in to hear what the child is asking for, I'll question the kid as if I didn't hear, "I'm sorry. What was the name of that toy again? Can you please say it a little louder for me?" When they enunciate, a wink to Mom and Dad conveys, *Did you get that?* If the folks aren't leaning in, it's just a cool breeze with the kid and me.

When we get to the end of our visit, I ask if I can keep the list. Of course, you and I both know the answer will be yes. It will *always* be yes. Why else would they go through all that trouble if they didn't want me to take their list back to the elves at the shop? The children don't want me to forget anything, especially them.

Still, I make a little production of the situation, slowly folding the list back up and carefully tucking it into my boot.

This frees up my hands, which are quickly extended back out for tickling.

I know some wishes are physically impossible (a live pony, a real helicopter, a unicorn). Still, I smile, nod my head, tousle their hair, and watch them skip off. When the parents see the gleeful skipping, oftentimes, they will turn and quietly mouth, "Thank you." I return the twinkle I just saw in their children's eyes. It brings adult tears—for me, too. It's all very touching.

By the end of the gig, I may have as many as a dozen lists in my boot.

Some, I keep. I have a nice collection. Some are lovely. Some are not. Some are crisp afternoons. Some are complete disasters.

In case you're wondering, yes, there is a file 13 on the North Pole.

10

Santa goes to the Ballet

One afternoon, only two days before Christmas, I headed to another wonderful venue and another jolly up. If you're wondering what Santa Claus has in common with the Nashville Ballet's Nutcracker Suite, so was I. They wanted Santa to appear.

For the final encore of the final performance of their long, holiday run, Santa was to make his presence known. He does this, while the ballerinas and ballerinos are still onstage, taking their final bows. The crowd is cheering and on their feet. By the time Santa makes the scene, he walks out to a standing ovation, already in progress.

I hadn't heard of any of this. But there you have it. A gig is a gig. This is a good one.

Once again, my real beard got me the gig. They specifically requested an authentic beard, so I fluffed it up, nicely. I know the house will be dancing up a storm. The final matinee before Christmas is always a jolly sellout. This one was no different.

I was asked to be ready by 4:30 for my 4:45 appearance, though the actual production started at 3:00. I wasn't needed, to fill Santa's five-minute slot, until right before the final curtain. Still, I arrived in plenty of time to relax, "Santa up," and "Santa out." I considered this to be quite a prestigious gig. I was going to be good and goofy and, most importantly, ready.

Plus, I wanted to experience the entire scope of the production and spend the day with the ballet. The anticipation was thrilling. It always is. I've always enjoyed the backstage bustle of a theatrical performance. Because of this, I try to turn every one of my musical gigs into a performance, no matter how small. I love all the bustle and the hustle and the tussle.

The Tennessee Performing Arts Center (TPAC) holds 947 people, with plenty of dressing rooms located directly below the stage. On this day, everyone had shown up in their holiday finest. I was led into the bowels of the building and into a long hallway with dressing rooms on either side.

With my vintage-green Santa suitcase in hand, I found my way to the very end of the hall. I was shown into a plush room, that served as both a green room and a dressing room and was occupied by staff, administrators, and retired dancers from days of ballet yore. They were all smiles when I walked in. They knew why I was there. Their greetings were holiday warm. Although I refrained from a holiday quaff, I was welcomed in and joined the merry mix.

As showtime neared, the others began to head up to their seats. I sat alone in the quieted room and slowly began the transformation. Boots and pants and suspenders were readied, even though I still had over an hour until my actual appearance.

Dressing rooms, up and down the hall, were full of dancers. The first few rooms were filled with women in various stage of costume, for various scenes coming up. Alongside them, were two rooms of men, making the same preparations. I went through the same process, putting on my bulky Santa pants.

Fat & Funny

The excitement was crackling, when the backstage announcement came over the intercom: "Scene 1. Stage right. Scene 2, twelve minutes." This sent everyone scurrying to mirrors, for final touch-ups.

While groups of women, dressed as Juliets, walked by and a group of men, dressed as Romeos followed, I just smiled and watched the parade. I had a pretty good view from my end of the hall.

When the curtain rose, I could hear the murmur of the crowd, through the floorboards. The full orchestra pit roared merriment into the air. A full orchestra can be quite loud. The place was as festive as can be.

This was the closing night of the troupe's run, which put an extra zip into the air, as closing nights always tend to do. Plus, all of this, happening only a couple days before Christmas, added to the gaiety. After twenty-three performances, the dancers were focused, razor sharp, and at the top of their game. They were also eager to end the run and get on with other things in their lives. The air was absolutely electric.

When the dancers headed out of sight, Santa was still at the end of the quiet hall. The play was on, and I still had an hour to wait. I had donned only my pants and boots, saving my coat and hat for the stage. This way, I could quickly look like him, with minimal preparation.

This time, I had planned ahead and brought a crossword-puzzle book with me, another of my favorite pastimes. When I commenced to reading and jotting, the dressing room area got quiet. The quiet lasted until the first girls came off stage, rushed to their dressing rooms, and began their wardrobe changes for the upcoming scenes. When the intercom announced, "Flower girls to the stage," another commotion stirred.

Due to my warm, stuffy, windowless dressing room, I had actually scooted a chair into the hallway, directly outside my door. The hallway was cooler. Old, fat guys like cooler much more than they like stuffier.

This put me at the far end of the hallway, with all the dressing-room commotion right in front of me. I saw primping dancers, heading to the stage and panting dancers returning.

These dancers were not only artists; they were athletes. Their physiques were magnificent. It was easy to tell that they were some of the finest dancers on the planet.

When they turned the far corner of the hall and saw Santa quietly sitting in a chair, doing a crossword puzzle, some rushed right over with cameras. Their smiles came directly from the stage. I didn't even have to stand up—they leaned in. They quickly came and went, as they dashed back to their dressing rooms.

Some of the others just look down their noses at me. This doesn't bother me. I don't mind. They have their gig; I got mine.

When intermission arrived, visitors came backstage, cramming the hallways with well-wishers, clamor, and chatter. I continued to just sit there, fielding the occasional photo request. I had no problem with any of this. If they didn't mind having their pictures taken with an old guy in his suspenders, doing a crossword puzzle, I didn't mind, either.

When the second act started, visitors headed back up to their seats, things returned to normal, and Santa returned to his eight-letter word for *surreal* at 17 Across.

Knowing that I would be called upon soon, I headed back to

my suitcase to retrieve my coat, gloves, and belt. In the middle of a dressing room, filled with very bright lighting, I put final, rosy touches to my cheeks and popped in a breath mint. I heard a knock on my door and then, "Santa, are you ready?"

My chaperone reassured me that there was still a little time, before I would actually go on. She also asked if I would like to see the grand finale from the wings. When I told her that I would love to, I quickly applied the final touches. She then led me up the staircase, through a side door, and into a very hushed, darkened stage-right wing.

Directly in front of me was the beautiful, breathtaking finale. The lighting was spectacular. The colors were brilliant. The orchestra was loud and robust, and the couple onstage were magnificent. I saw everyone, cast and crew, coming around the far turn of their Preakness and heading for the finish line.

While the rest of the cast eagerly waited in the wings, for final bows and curtain calls, they barely stifled tears of excitement. As the onstage dancers flawlessly executed their moves—I must admit—they brought me to tears, as well.

The audience leapt to their feet. The curtain went down. Applause was thunderous. I quietly stood in the wings.

Then, the curtain rose. The orchestra throbbed. The pair took another bow, and the curtain came down.

The entire cast then took the stage, and the curtain went back up. The audience clapped and cheered even louder.

Once again, I had been instructed about what they wanted me—I mean, Santa—to do: 1) saunter onstage, 2) do not rush about, 3) smile, 4) make merry, and 5) wave to the children in the crowd.

Then, my guide instructed me to just slowly sidle my way to

the other side of the stage, over the course of the song. I found this to be kind of weird. I asked if she really wanted me to just loiter and meander right in front of these beautiful dancers. When she grinned and emphatically nodded her head, a-sidling I went.

After the second wave of bows, the orchestra kicked back up into "We Wish You a Merry Christmas." Because I was stationed directly behind the curtain, when she said, "Go," I went. I began sauntering and loitering.

When I hit the stage, I waved my arms and led the crowd in song. They were already on their feet, giving the wonderful dance troupe a standing ovation. They began to sing, as I ambled about the stage, jingled my little bell, and started waving my ass off.

Right in the middle of all this pastoral beauty, there I stood—a large, red pimple, smack-dab in the middle of the nutcracker's forehead.

After the first stanza, I looked over my shoulder and saw an absolutely spectacular sight. In the middle of the stage, awash in brilliant orange, blue, pink, and green, stood the entire cast, still in choreographed position.

Their posture was perfect, as I continued to clomp around. When I tossed my hands up, in recognition to them, the audience surged. They sang even louder, as I wandered downstage and into the fringes of the spotlight. I also turned to the dancers and joined in the applause. I clapped as loud as my muffled gloves would allow.

Then, I returned my attention back to the kids in the audience. I did my own little jig and meandered toward stage left. By doing this jig, I can truthfully say that I danced with the ballet.

But it was time to shine the light back onto the real dancers. This was still their time. They had been dancing their asses off for an hour and a half. I'd been onstage for almost two minutes.

As the second stanza of the song finished, the dancers began to let down their hair and their stances. Many began flowing and waving to the crowd. Tears appeared. Flowers appeared. Hugs abounded.

As the third and final stanza rolled around, I prompted the crowd to sing even louder. They did, just that. I had 'em in the palm of my glove.

A quiet stagehand, positioned directly behind the curtain to my immediate left whispered, "Watch yourself, Santa. Heads up. Curtain coming in." I looked up and stepped back, out of the way. The curtain slowly lowered and landed four feet in front of my face. The dancers started embracing and embracing and embracing some more. Their sense of relief was profound.

I could still hear the rustle of the mingling crowd, buzzing through the thick curtain. I turned around to take one last look at the magnificent stage. I could only stand in awe—but only for a minute. For those sixty seconds, I felt like I was on peyote, watching a Grateful Dead light show in the middle of an episode of *The Twilight Zone*.

Then, my chaperone quickly took me by the hand, and we rushed out to the bustling lobby, still filled with an excited, exiting crowd. I positioned myself, smack-dab in the middle of the path to the door. Everyone was glowing with spirit. When I jingled my jingle bell, the children heard it and gathered at my feet.

With everyone in such a good mood, it was effortless to take warmhearted photos. These kids were all dressed up, which also added to the festivity. They weren't sloppy kids, dragging their baggy pants to the mall. These were snappy kids, going to the theater. No hunting boots and backward baseball hats here. It was refreshing.

By the matinee's end, it was nearing five o'clock. The evening was still relatively young, and most folks were in a rush to get to a party, go shopping, or just head to their fireplaces. I welcomed everyone who wanted to cuddle up for a few seconds and take a snapshot.

Because everyone was in such a holiday hurry, the place cleared in fewer than thirty minutes. As the last stragglers exited the lobby, I was led back across the empty, flood-lit stage—now filled with stagehands, quietly disassembling the set. Then, it was back downstairs to my dressing room.

Once there, I assured my chaperone that I would be fine and could navigate my way out of the building. She was grateful. She thanked me, shook my hand, handed me a check, and rushed off into her Sunday evening.

Some straggling dancers made a few photo requests, as everyone was still in adrenaline mode. They were also in 'I just want to get the hell out of here' mode.

They had done twenty-three performances. They had taken off the grease paint for the last time. They were ready to hit the road, so hit the road, they did.

After a few minutes, the place was completely empty, leaving nothing but an echoing hallway and a janitor quietly rolling a trash can, a handful of wardrobe people, quietly collecting and sorting costumes, and me, quietly taking off my coat and pants.

Fat & Funny

After the din of the previous few hours, the concrete silence was deafening. I also knew that it was only late afternoon and I really didn't have anything else on my agenda. So, I headed home and had a nice dinner and a glass of wine with Julie. That's always a pleasant way to end a pleasant day.

I put Santa back into his green suitcase and slowly walked back down the quiet corridor. I looked around and gazed at the show posters and photos of past dancers. Although I did not find my photo on the wall—and probably never will—I let out a resounding chuckle and sigh.

How absurd is all this? I thought. I just did a jig for a buck, onstage with the ballet. I guess that actually affirms me as a professional dancer. Now, my resumé, can contain "Danced with the Nashville Ballet."

I walked past the security guard at the stage door and out into the quiet dusk. People walked by, arm in arm. Streetlights flashed. Taxis streamed by. The wind blew a winter breeze. I pulled up my collar, grabbed my suitcase, and walked into the night.

Yep, a professional dancer, I am. I just did *The Nutcracker.*

11

House Concerts

"'T was the night before Christmas, and all through the house …"

My gigs on Christmas Eve were the last two of the year. They were also a couple of the easiest of the season. I was hired to make brief, personal visits (thirty minutes each) to kids in the comfort of their homes, on the evening of December 24. Once again, I don't mind working on my birthday.

Although the two gigs were different, they followed the same template: ring the doorbell, walk in, stomp around for half an hour, play with the kids, and take pictures with them. Then, tell everyone how busy you are and vanish into the Christmas Eve night.

Even though I use the same game plan, the latter gig is for an only child of a very affluent family, quietly awaiting in their mansion. Because of the later start time, this means the child will be that much closer to bedtime. The earlier appearance was for eight loud, Pepsied-up kids and their extended families. The screaming was at a fever pitch. The place was anything but subdued.

By Christmas Eve, all of Santa's seeds have been strewn and sown. The crops have been fertilized, anticipation is at an all-time high, and tomorrow is harvest day. Only one more night of anxious sleep for these kids.

Gigs like this are usually not in downtrodden neighborhoods

or trailer parks, where folks can't afford a few extra bucks for a personal visit from him. They're in neighborhoods with checkbooks, budgets, bank accounts, and big garages.

Appearance times are prearranged. I make advance phone calls to doting grandparents, who are eager to see the smiling faces of their grandchildren, when Santa walks into the room. They have no qualms about ponying up.

The phone calls are made, to coordinate the 'where', 'when', and 'how'. If time allows, like this particular day, one appearance can easily be dovetailed into a second, before the curtain comes down on another holiday season.

When I pulled up to the first house, I was fully dressed and sat in my darkened truck. The logistics were all worked out, beforehand. Depending on the number of children, things can get more entailed. But, not much.

Another asset of this time of year, is that it gets dark early, which is good for the stealth element. It also affords the chance to make it to a second gig, before the evening gets too late.

The night's first gig was for eight kids—siblings, cousins, and neighbors. When I met the liaisons on the darkened porch, I was handed a sack with presents for each of the kids. When I informed them that I would be leaving as soon as I walked back out the door, I received my envelope.

Inside, I could hear the screeching of the kids. With a hearty meal and a couple cookies in them, they were as revved up and excited as kids can get, at this time of year. With sack in hand, I told my liaisons to head back inside, rejoin the party, like nothing was happening, and wait for a few minutes. I would ring the doorbell and we'd be off to the races.

They walked back inside. I stood in the dark.

After several moments, I rang the doorbell. The screeching turned to outright screaming. I heard the patter of sixteen little feet, dashing for the door. When they threw it open, shrieks erupted. Several of the kids were so excited, all they could do was hop up and down, uncontrollably. The rug in the foyer seemed like a trampoline.

I tried to match them in volume, as I tried to belly laugh over their din. Then, I stomped in and hugged them all. Some stayed aloof, not wanting anything to do with the hugging part. I swung them around, shook hands with every adult, and switched on the Santa machine.

Then, I meandered my way to the Christmas tree, where the family had arranged for me to sit. I dragged out this part of the show. I also dragged along the kids' anticipation of what could be in my sack. I like to think of these as lessons in patience.

I winked at the grown-ups. I played with the kids.

After a few, brief moments, I settled into my chair and began idle chatter with the children. Simple questions have simple answers:

"Have you been good this year?" "Yay!"

"Who's excited about tomorrow?" "Meeeeee!"

When they asked if I needed anything, my request for a simple glass of water and a cookie, sent some of the kids scurrying to the kitchen. This can be considered just another stalling tactic, if you wish.

After I chit-chatted with everyone for several minutes, I slowly began to open the sack. The kids held their breath as they inched closer. Each name was read, and each present was presented. Each child overflowed with joy at the sight of his or her toy.

Fat & Funny

Cameras flashed, as wrapping paper was flung into whirlwinds of color. As the contents of my sack were gifted out, all focus shifted away from me. I just sat back, as the family interacted and embraced one another. I watched, not only the party in the room, but also the clock on the wall. I had another gig to get to.

After a few minutes, it was picture time. Because I had been hanging out for ten or fifteen minutes, none of the kids were too freaked out by my presence, anymore. Plus, I had just handed them toys. They jumped right up into my lap and whispered into my ear. We all smiled for Grandma's camera.

After all the kids have sat with Santa individually, each family wanted its own portrait with him. Then, they wanted one with all the aunts and uncles. Then, they wanted one with only the boys and one with only the girls. Then, they wanted one with the pets. Then, they wanted one with—well, you get the picture.

I didn't have a problem with any of this. A hundred and fifty pictures would be taken, and I'd be right in the center of all of them. I'd also be the center of attention in *none* of them. The smiles on those little faces are what folks wanted to see, not me. I patiently sat and took every photo. It's part of the gig.

After picture time, the kids were pretty much done with Santa. Although the air was still filled with cheer and music, the party tempered. Some of the kids started to wander back into what they were doing, before I showed up.

I took this time to hang out and chat with the adults. They were amused and curious about my gig, asking questions about being a Santa, how often I appear, and so on. With all the kids in the other rooms, I talked of my cottage industry. I also told them about how much fun it is.

As we mingled, I was offered cocktails and beer. I politely declined every offer. Beer breath is not a very good Santa trait. An offer I never decline, though, is a host's offer to make me a plate of food, for later.

As the gig neared its end, I began to slowly shuffle toward the door. I yelled to the kids, one last time, and they rumbled down the steps for final goodbye hugs.

I reminded everyone to leave me one cookie and only a half a glass of milk. As I went into a long, drawn-out explanation about how I don't have time to drink a whole glass of milk and can only eat one cookie and blah, blah, blah, the kids were all ears and nods. One last wave and burst of holiday cheer, got me out the door, back into the darkness, and around the corner to my truck.

With forty-five minutes until my next appearance, I leisurely sat and ate the plate of food (these are always holiday good) and a cookie. This gets a reindeer motor runnin'. We're off, and I make my way across town, to the next gig—I mean, house.

I made it to the next home and positioned my truck for a quick exit. I called in to the party, letting my contact know that I was outside. The waiting began. Is the waiting, the hardest part? Not really. I don't mind waiting. To be a gig Santa, it helps to be a patient guy.

Surprising an only child is much easier than dealing with a rowdy clan. Once again, I was met by an uncle on the dark porch, where I can remain out of sight. I gathered last-minute details—the child's name, interests, pets, favorite things to do, and so on. This way, when I walk in, I can make it appear that

Fat & Funny

I already know everything about the child, like a good Santa should.

When I was a young lad, Paul Bunyan used this same trick on me, when my family summer vacationed in Brainerd, Minnesota. Yes, Brainerd, Minnesota. Other families take childhood fantasy trips to Disney Land. We took childhood fantasy trips to Paul Bunyan Land.

When we walked in the front gate, a gigantic lumberjack structure would loom and look down, bellow our names, and welcome us from St. Louis. I hadn't noticed my mother, filling out information sheets about us. We could not believe that Paul Bunyan already knew our names. We were sucked right in. I use this same tactic, today.

When I do gigs at this late hour, if the child isn't getting too tired, I can walk in the door, whenever they want me to. I have no problem, pushing showtime up twenty minutes. If they want me to hand the child a present, I make sure it's wrapped and readied. If they want to set up for photos, a chair should be set by the tree. They understand all of this. It's not rocket surgery, folks.

As in the earlier gig, I informed the adults to head back to the party, act like nothing was out of the ordinary, and get ready to answer the doorbell. At this point, once again, I was left alone in the dark with my sack, filled with one toy. Inside, I heard muffled conversations. After several minutes, I rang the doorbell. I could hear the gasp of the adults and the squeal of the child. Both were exhilarating.

When the door was answered, I stepped into the room and acted like I was in a hurry. After all, it was Christmas Eve. Santa still had a lot of work to do. But I was there now, so we needed to make good use of our time.

When I saw the child, I squinted my eyes, rubbed my chin, and feigned contemplation—but, not for too long. When I called out the child's name, his eyes burst into saucers (just as mine did, when Paul Bunyan bellowed my name).

I made sure that everyone in the room received greetings and handshakes. But when it came to greeting the child, one on one, he received undivided attention.

I asked for a small glass of orange juice, which the little one scampered off to retrieve. When the child disappeared into the kitchen, exclaiming, "Santa wants some orange juice!" I turned to the adults. They laughed and asked if I wanted some vodka in my juice. We shared grins. They were ecstatic.

When the child returned with the cool liquid, the games began. I started with light banter, peppered with all the information I had received earlier on the porch. If kids like Spider-man, I let them tell me all about Spider-man. If they like Barbies, I let them tell me all about Barbies. And if they like football, I let them tell me all about football. I just sit and listen. It's still not rocket surgery.

Before it got too late, I let the adults know that we should quickly take photos, while the kid was still not too tired. They could capture the look of astonishment, while it was still fresh on the child's face.

Hair is combed. Shirt collars are straightened. Santa's lap is occupied. Photos are taken and digitally approved, right on the spot. Then, it was time to goof off. I made small talk with the child, as well as the grown-ups. I share a few silly jokes and a couple of stories about Rudolph. Basically, I joined their party.

Fat & Funny

When it came time to see the contents of my sack, I opened it wide and handed the child his gift. The shredding of wrapping paper was much more subdued, than it had been at my earlier gig. Still, it was no less euphoric.

Cameras flashed, as I sat off to the side. After the gift was unwrapped, I strolled over to a comfortable chair, by a comfortable, roaring fireplace, half expecting to see Andy Williams and Claudine Longet appear.

When I asked the child to bring me his favorite book, he dashed down the hall and returned in a flash. He hopped into the chair with me, and we began to read. As we settled in, the adults got candid photos. The chaos of the first party was replaced with the calm crackling of hickory.

After everyone was satisfied with their photos, I feigned a yawn, directed my attention to the child, and went into my familiar repertoire: "Wow. It's getting late. I guess I should get going. I've got lots of houses to visit tonight, and *you'd* better go to sleep." I shook the grandpa's hand. He slipped me the holly.

Once again, I asked the child to leave me only one cookie and a half glass of milk. As I headed toward the door, I tell him that he'd better start getting ready for bed. As I headed out the door, he headed off to sleep.

I got to my truck and took off my hat, gloves, and coat. Then, it was back to the house for a quiet, birthday evening. When I walked in the door, a stiff margarita was a great way to end a very nice and chaotic Santa season.

Viva la Kringle.

12
Mrs. Claus

"A happy wife, a happy life," someone once said. "Ain't nobody happy, if Mama ain't happy," someone else said.

"Mama tried," said Merle Haggard.

Ladies and gentlemen, it's time to turn the spotlight onto my better half. That's right. Let's hear it for (drum roll, please) Mrs. Claus!

Sadly, being a professional Santa is an option, only open to males. So, ladies, this chapter is for you. If you want to try your hand at being Mrs. Claus, her gig is a whole other reindeer game. It's also just as easy and just as much fun.

Sometimes, a party planner will request a Santa *and* a Mrs. Santa. If there are two clauses written into their budget, two Clauses show up.

Guys. In real life, if your wife isn't bumpy and frumpy and slappy and happy, you'll have to find someone, who is. Many slappy, happy women are married to men, who are neither. Most of these guys aren't the least bit interested in any of this shit.

They are not round. They are not rosy. They are not fat. They are not funny, and they don't have beards.

A lot of men aren't even close to Santa's stature. There's no way a slim man, standing five-feet, one-inch tall, can resemble a roly-poly oaf. Sorry, littler guys.

The same goes for the gals. My wife, Julie, could never be a convincing Mrs. Claus. She's a slender five feet, two inches, with no trace of a white bun anywhere near her hair.

Chunky ladies may be bumpy and frumpy. Many have hubbies who are just plain grumpy. If a man doesn't resemble Santa, he just doesn't—period. Santa doesn't have short, thinning black hair. That's just how it goes. Sorry.

Ladies, if you're tan and slim and trim in a yellow polka-dot bikini, being Mrs. Claus is probably out of the question for you. But if you fit the jolly description, and your spouse isn't holly or jolly, this shouldn't hinder you from stuffing a few extra bucks into your stocking. I know several women who easily fill the role of Mrs. Claus. They're lovely women with lovely smiles and healthy senses of humor. They're adorable actresses and a barrel of monkeys to hang around with. Children love them.

Over the course of the gig, the kids will pay me a short visit, but they *love* hanging around and playing with "me missus." It's nice to watch these women enjoy being Mrs. C, as much as I enjoy being Mr. C.

Sadly, though, there aren't as many gigs available for Mrs. C. But, when they arise, these women add a cozy, down-home feel to each and every scene they spin. It's a joy to see.

It doesn't matter that you and Mrs. Claus aren't related. No one will ever know that the two of you aren't really spouses. No one needs to know. A gig is a gig. Remember?

The two of you show up as a pair. You portray yourselves as a pair. You chuckle and eat cookies and drink milk with the kids as a pair. Then you get your checks and wave goodbye as a pair, and finally leave the building and disappear as a pair.

Once outside, if you have another gig booked, you may talk

logistics. Then, you just bid each other a fond farewell and drive off in different directions.

All of these women are wonderfully Mrs. Claus-ish and wonderfully young at heart. Every one of them is effervescent and a complete pro to work with. Every one of them is holly and jolly to be around.

They do most of the work, anyway. While she jollies about, hands out cookies, wipes up spilled milk, sings songs, and reads stories, I just watch from my couch, like a bump on a log. I love to see these gals have such a good time, playing with the children.

Not so long ago, they were mothers, with little children of their own. You can tell, not only were they good mothers, they were good *mommies*. Most still miss their mommy days. You can't blame them. I still miss my daddy days, too.

Many have grandchildren they can dote on, but this gig gives them another chance to snuggle and giggle for a couple of hours. Then, they just wave goodbye and leave, with a few coins in their purses.

When a beautiful child wants to snuggle with her, that child is royally snuggled. Merry conversations begin. Many of the children want to snuggle up to me, too. That's all right. I don't mind. I've got a big, soft suit on, and I can snuggle and giggle as well as my fake spouse.

When Mrs. Claus interacts, children are magnetically drawn to her. They gather at her feet. She sweeps them up in her apron and swings them around, like the basket ride at a county fair.

Her station is usually near mine, somewhere in the vicinity of the Christmas tree. I'm just sitting there. My area is clean and devoid of random things. Her area, on the other hand, is completely cluttered with books and crayons and knitting and cookie crumbs and milk and mittens and tissue paper.

These ladies arrive to the gig with large handbags, filled with a myriad of soft, crafty, comforting things. Even if they don't get any knitting done, the mere sight of it, sitting in their laps, is calming. The blankets they use to snuggle, smell clean and fresh. They also keep Mrs. Claus nice and warm, as they cover their laps.

When the gig is over, Mrs. Claus just tosses her blanket and her books back into her bag. She is quickly ready to leave, and so am I.

We fling one last flurry of holiday kisses into the air. Along with a "Ho, ho, ho" and a "Hugs galore," we head for our sleighs. Then, we fly back to the North Pole. Eh, you know what I mean. We just drive back to our houses.

Not every gig, though, is a Mrs. Claus gig. Sometimes, she can feel quite out of place, when it just *ain't* her gig. I'll explain.

Mrs. Santa doesn't like late-night drunk fests. She's more of a hot chocolate, morning person. She likes to go to sleep and wake up when the children do, just like most fogies our age.

When I'm booked for a late-night Christmas bash, I know Mrs. Claus probably won't be there. Mama's frump and joy would just be wasted on a bunch of yahoos with Bluetooths, beards, tattoos, skinny jeans, brown shoes, and pierced noses and eyebrows.

I also know, Mrs. Claus would just as soon not hang out with the hipster crowd. Most of the time, I don't even want to hang out with the hipster crowd.

Her frump and joy would also be wasted on young, texting

girls in tight, red skirts with red lipstick rings on their cigarettes and martini glasses. These scarlets don't have a whole lot in common with Mrs. C, or her red apron. They don't really want to hang out with an old lady, anyway. Well, guess what, Tiffany? Mrs. Claus really, really, *really* doesn't want to hang out with you, either. Watching these gals stumble around on their high heels can be amusing for me, but not for Mrs. C.

Many of these party girls get stinking hammered and can't wait to hit the dance floor. There, I watch them bumble and mumble their way through, "Sweet Caroline—*bom, bom, bom.*"

If each gal had a third arm, there would be no problem. Then, they wouldn't have to fumble with their cocktails, their cigarettes, and their cell phones. Plus, some of these gals get just as loud, belligerent, and crude as their male counterparts. It's not a pretty sight.

Some old men like to flirt with these young girls. I find them to be boring. Chasing them would be futile and a complete waste of time. It's like the adage of the old dog, who finally catches the bus tire he's been chasing. Once you catch it, what are you going to do with it?

Although gigs with Mrs. Claus are less frequent, they do occur. When I learn that a gig will include a female co-star, I know it will be warm and fuzzy. Every lady I've worked with has been warm, fuzzy and a ton of fun to hang out with.

Elves, on the other hand, are a whole, different animal. All you have to do, to be an elf is, be little (not dumpy), be perky (not frumpy), and be alert. All three traits are *musts* for an elf.

Like you probably did, I laughed myself silly at Will Ferrell in *Elf*. This gig, though, is for a smaller human. It's also a good gig for a diminutive, agile woman or a cheerful girl with a cheerleader laugh. These ladies are also fine actresses, in little green suits with pointy shoes and pointy hats. Perky—remember? The gig—remember?

Elves are energetic. Elves are affable and convivial. They are also quite valuable, especially at mall gigs, when the line to see Santa winds out the door to the parking lot. Elves are worth their weight in green and red piping.

Elves should know how to efficiently and quickly move folks onto my lap, across the stage, and off to the exit. Crowd control is an asset for my little helpers. Unfortunately, their gigs are almost as scarce as those for Mrs. Claus.

Most of the time, an elf is provided by mall management. Sometimes, there are multiple elves. The administration's report already knows how many people should be passing through. They also know how unruly a long line of tired, hungry kids can get. Oftentimes, elves are just employees from the front office, who have a way with people and know how to herd and move them along.

No one is given the bum's rush, though. Malls like to make sure every child gets their fair share of my time and a smiling picture, like clockwork. I like that, too. But with an eye on the queue, an elf can make things flow smoother and quicker. Like an assembly line, the next visitors are readied and brought up in a flash.

Elves and Mrs. Claus play very nice and essential roles in the scenes we set. Not only are they performing valuable roles, they're performing valuable tasks. Our little area becomes our little stage, and we become the actors. Our cast of two is always a jolly roster.

Still, Santa is the main focus. At first glance, it may appear that my accomplices are just fooling around and goofing off. They are not. Nothing could be further from the truth. Every member of the team is important. That's why it's called a *team effort.*

Everyone takes a bow. The curtain comes down. We vanish into thin air.

While I play the big guy, my fellow cast members play little people and old ladies. All, are important roles.

My gigs may be more in demand, but a good Mrs. Claus and a good elf are worth their weight in cookies.

13
Older Gals Like Santa, Too

The ringing of the telephone shattered the quiet, summer morning. Outside my window, the heat index was already a sweltering 91 degrees. Hardly a Santa situation.

But I picked up the phone. Imagine that. In this modern world, someone still answers the telephone. Oddly enough, that's what old guys do. They answer their phones.

A very close friend, who is also a musician and confirmed bachelor was on the other end, laughing heartily. "Supe, you're not going to believe this," he said with a laugh.

"Try me. I'm always up for a good chuckle," I replied.

He continued, "I just logged onto one of those online dating sites. I saw this woman. She seemed really nice. Her profile looked cool, and she was pretty sharp-looking. Then, when I began leafing through her photo section, there she was, sitting on Santa's lap—and *you* were the Santa."

Laughter pealed from both ends of that phone line. It was a funny morning. Of course, I had no idea or recollection of who he was talking about. Absolutely none. But there it was—proof, in black and white and red.

Every girl, no matter how old she is, loves having her picture taken with Santa Claus. A fact is a fact. Don't complain. When you're Santa, girls of all ages want to sit on your lap, ranging from six weeks, to sixty-six years and six weeks.

Plus, remember, there are only two columns on Santa's list: nice and naughty. I have corresponding banter and a separate set of jokes for both sides of this coin. Interactions can be fun, and they're usually pretty funny.

The following groups of gals shape up, more or less, as follows:

a) Infants: I'm not really sure if they're excited to see me, or not. It's hard to tell. Some of them are so tiny, they have no idea what's happening. Some don't even wake up from their slumber. Others are merely bundles. All I do is hold them up to the camera, smile, and hand them right back. Children, who are a little bit older, are excited to see me. In the eyes of a two-year-old, my myth lives on. I can see it in their baby teeth smile.

b) Preteens: They're excited, but not quite as much as younger kids. Santa's myth has definitely been debunked. Many still teeter between becoming a lady and remaining a girl. Though most are moving onward and upward, to better things, they're still quite pleasant and, on many occasions, quite childlike.

c) Teens: Teenagers are pretty much, hit or miss. Some can still be cheery, lovely, and full of spark, while some just roll their eyes. "Whatever", they utter. "If Tammy's gonna take her picture, I guess I will too." Others can't be bothered. They just want to hang out in the parking lot with their boyfriends, twirl their hair, and smoke cigarettes. This is also the age, where they start deciding whether to place themselves on the nice list or the naughty list. They can go either way.

d) Twenties and thirties: If life is treating them well, they are young at heart and as cheerful as can be. If life hasn't dealt them a very good hand, they may not be quite as cozy and rosy. If a messy divorce, a brood of kids, bouncing alimony checks, and a repossessed pick-up truck are involved, attitudes and outlooks can go haywire, quite rapidly.

e) Forties and fifties: These women are carbon copies of those in the previous section, but with more jewelry.

f) Sixties: –For these women, time is beginning to take its toll. This is not a gender-specific issue; lots of older men are well into this phase of life, too. Those without the money for nipping and tucking have started bagging and sagging around the edges. If alcohol and tobacco enter the equation, you can add wrinkling to the mix. Still, most of these gals are lovely, touch-of-gray women, who just want to doll up and go see Santa.

g) Seventies and up: Now, they're starting to reach Santa's age group, and the jolly old man is looking pretty good to them. Many are stately, demure women who aren't averse to a little harmless flirting. They twinkle and bat their eyes. I compliment them on their outfits. This sets their hearts aflutter. Others can be quite haggard in their Dale Earnhardt sweatshirts.

Every girl or woman, in every one of these categories, has one thing in common with the others: She wants her picture taken with Santa, while she tells him what she wants for Christmas.

All of this, got me to thinking about some of the older, bawdier women who have visited and some of their odder, bawdier requests. I could write a book.

Young girls with auburn curls are one thing. They're wonderful. Their innocent glee abounds, as they playfully jump about and onto my lap. We snuggle and talk a lot, laughing all the way. Grown women are another story. Actually, there are a million stories.

There are short ones and long ones (the stories, not the gals). There are thin ones and round ones (the gals, not the stories). There are loud ones, sullen ones, prim and proper ones, angry ones, lonely ones, and drunken ones.

When I watch them approach, I can look right into their eyes and pretty much predict what's going to happen for the next several minutes.

Some, come with fun.
Some, come with frowns.
Some, come with stories.
Some, come with long stories.
Some, come with extremely long stories.
Some, come with fancy perfumes.
Some, come reeking of gin and Marlboros.
Some, come with daddy issues.

All, of course, come with their smiles, their sway, and their wish lists for Santa.

Some are with their husbands and boyfriends. Every girl will want her picture taken, even if her dour counterpart wants nothing to do with me. Begrudgingly, he may step into the photo, but this is definitely her show.

Fat & Funny

Some spunky, old guys just can't wait to jump into the frame with their spunky, old wives. When this happens, things can really get funny, in a flash. I do absolutely nothing to hinder or hurry these folks away. Henny Youngman jokes and Jerry Lewis routines break out, on the spot. Often, the guys' watches sparkle as much as their wives.

Sometimes, they will inconspicuously slip a little cash into Santa's glove. Santa loves it, when this happens. Three cheers for spunky, old guys. A lot of times, I consider myself a spunky, old guy.

But most gals just want to talk, vent, seethe, confide, or flirt. I begin each visit with, "Hello, my dear. Merry Christmas. Come up and talk to me."

1. You must be careful about what you wish for. Some gals just want to talk and talk and talk. I don't mind—I'm on the clock. Just as I do with the young kids, I let the old gals set the pace and direction of the conversation. I get to hear about their children, their grandchildren, and their great-grandchildren. I have no problem with this. I can relate. I have seven grandkids of my own, of whom I'm very proud. Others stop by with one, simple request: "Santa, I want a *man*."

2. Others want to start right in with, "All I want for Christmas is for my aunt to mind her own g—d---- business and stop bothering everybody, especially Mom. Nobody else in the family can stand her. We've tried talking to her a million times, but blah, blah, blah. Blah, blah, blah. *Blah, blah, blah.*" I just sit and smile and glance up at the clock.

3. "You know what I really want for Christmas?" one lady fumed. "I want you to kick that no-good, son-of-a-bitch husband of mine in the balls. If he wants to sleep with that little hussy, I'll yank every bleach-blond hair out of her empty, little head. You know what they did? Blah, blah, blah. Then, he walked back into the trailer and blah, blah, blah, acting like a blah, blah, blah, blah, blah."

   After the seething (i.e., as soon as she stops to catch her breath and before she can pick up where she left off), I quickly dive into my most diplomatic, "Okay. So, let's look over there and smile for that camera. Here we go. Three, two, one. *Cheese*. Merry Christmas." Then, I dive directly into my subtle old-man, get-off-my-lap routine.

4. Some quietly walk up and give me a sheepish hug, before meekly sidling in. I have seen some lonely women, in this frame of mind. I can tell that they just want to sit and talk to a man for a while, especially Santa Claus.

   I can also recognize daddy issues. When I let them start their tales, oftentimes they include loneliness as a child or awkwardness as a teen. I hear stories of abandonment as a spouse, with no desire to seek romance ever again. I see the sullenness and solitude. I quietly sit.

   I may be cheaper than a psychiatrist, but all I can offer is a smile, a friendly chat, and a sincere hug. Hopefully, this garners a return smile. Then, after our brief visit, I send them back into their lonely worlds.

5. "Santa, you're looking pretty damn handsome there, dude," another feisty, old lady began. "That beard looks so soft. Lemme feel it on mah face. Ooh, yeah. It's soft, all right." If the old gal doesn't have a husband or a boyfriend in the vicinity, things can get raunchy. The language can get pretty salty.

She *may* be all bark and no bite. That's one thing. But when they slip their phone numbers into your hand and whisper their hotel room numbers into your ear, that's another thing. Respond to absolutely none of it. As they sit beside me, their ramblings can veer off into multitudes of awkward, disjointed directions. Plus, these gals are my age, and I know how scatterbrained I can be. I have to chuckle at all of them, no matter how weird. After all, I am Santa.

Often, my smile and laughter are directed toward the next folks in line (even if the old gal, sitting beside me is giving her best Phyllis Diller impersonation).

No matter her age, when she walks away, I want her to feel better about herself and the world.

No matter her mood, when she walks away, I want her to feel better about herself and the world.

No matter her story, when she walks away, I want her to feel better about herself and the world.

It's what Santa does.

14

Double Duty and Double D's

I was pulling double duty, one mid-December Saturday. Traditionally, such days are very good for a Santa. If logistics will allow, a third gig can be squeezed in, for maximum Claus and a good day, payday. Today's two gigs, could not have been more different. One was for children. The other was for adults. They did, though, contain one, odd thing in common. The day began.

My first appearance was a midmorning (9:00–11:00) Christmas party for the well-groomed, well-mannered children of a well-mannered preschool in a well-groomed suburb. (The school and burb will remain anonymous. Santa doesn't remember so well, anyway.)

My second appearance would be that evening (8:00–12:00) at a drunken corporate Christmas party in a funky art space, with some not-so-well-mannered adults. (The name of the company will also remain anonymous. After this party, believe me, no one remembered anything.)

Now, for the oddity the two gigs had in common: At each, I had an AASS (Awkward Adult Santa Situation). Ho. Ho. Ho. Here we go.

Fat & Funny

That chilly morning, when I arrived at the preschool, the parking lot was empty. The halls and classrooms were quiet. The director of the school and her small staff were frantically putting their final touches on the community room, as well as the large tree standing next to the small stage.

That's right—a stage, complete with thick, plush curtains. Most preschool centers can't afford to build a stage. Affluent preschool centers can. They also can afford the large, ornate throne they had rented for me.

Although it was a party at heart, the main gist of this gig was to get photos of Timmy and Tammy with Santa. I like these gigs. All I have to do is sit there, laugh with the kids, and get them to smile for the cameras.

I parked my truck near the back of the school, for immediate departure. This is not because I don't want to hang around. The one who doesn't want to hang around is, well, Santa. He's a busy man. He (as well as *we*) has a mystique to uphold. I made this point clear to the school staff in advance, explaining that my disappearing act was not out of disrespect. It was for the youngsters. They don't need to see Santa, hanging around afterward, being a regular guy out of costume and eating a ham sandwich. Remember? The mystique.

I was led to one of the quiet, vacant classrooms in the back of the building, where I slowly transformed into him under the shadow of a SpongeBob SquarePants poster. I started to dress. As I glanced up at the giant circus clock on the wall, I could watch Santa time slowly approach. I could also see out the classroom window to the parking lot, which was beginning to fill with waves of Mercedes, BMWs, and large SUVs.

For the children, who attend this school on a daily basis, this was their Super Bowl. They knew right where they were going (familiar territory), and they knew they were going to see Santa Claus (every kid's dream).

They excitedly jumped from their cars in their Christmas finest. Hair was neatly combed, and clothes were wrinkle-free. Bejeweled mothers and grandmothers were accompanied by dads and granddads with gold chains, gold watches, and slacks.

I continued to sit in the quiet classroom and read the sports section of the paper. My time drew near.

When my time really was near, I stopped by the bathroom, since I had two hours of sitting ahead of me. My bladder was emptied and my cheeks rosied. Breath was minted. Belt was tightened. White gloves were pulled on. Time to go to work.

As I strolled up the quiet hallway—which was cordoned off, to keep me out of sight—I heard the hum and hubbub of the party. I strolled up to the back side of the curtain and bellowed, "Ho, ho, ho" down the echo-y hallway.

I heard the anticipation sweep across the room. Things settled. I remained silent and invisible. The party resumed. After twenty seconds, I issued another gregarious, "Ho, ho, ho" and made my entrance.

When I strolled through the curtain, I was greeted with wide eyes. I began waving to everyone and shaking hands with the teachers and parents. This gave the kids a few minutes to catch their breath and get used to the big red spectacle in the room.

Then, I turned to the children and chortled, as I held my belly and climbed onto my throne. There, I would spend the next couple of hours, quietly talking to the kids and, *more importantly*, listening to them.

They spewed forth. It was beautiful. Christmas lists were

recited, as well as those silly, random thoughts children always seem to come up with. I just sat there, smiling and listening. There is the occasional screamer, but most of the kids are well mannered and eager to jump into my lap and talk.

As for the screamers, they scream. If they're screamers, they're going to scream. Some come around, as I've gotten pretty good at talking to and calming children. I don't mind. Put them on my lap. If they scream, take the picture--quick. Then, get them off my lap--quick.

This day, though, most of the kids were pretty well adjusted. It was a very pleasant, relaxed morning. It was during this pleasant morning, when AASS # 1 took place.

After a morning of fancy, schmantzy women, walking their lovely, dovely children up to see me, one blatantly schmantzy cougar caught her high heel on the edge of the stage. Her jewelry rattled as she propelled across it—directly at me.

When she did, her grandson gently rolled up to my feet. Luckily, neither was hurt. She lunged forward, but caught herself before she completely face-planted. In that split instant, I involuntarily exclaimed, "Ohh!"

It all happened in such a flash, that I was of no help to either of them. As I exclaimed, "Ohh!" one of her perky, store-bought breasts leapt from her loose sweater and into plain view. As my dad would say, "You're gonna put somebody's eye out with that thing." She quickly gained her balance and readjusted herself.

Although the topic wasn't addressed, when I looked at her, she smiled. Her grin let Santa know that she was quite proud of them, and had no problem with him, gazing at her rack of reindeer. I had exclaimed, simply because she had stumbled. The boob shot was an added bonus.

No one else in the room saw, or realized what had just taken place. But she did, and I did. The visit was pleasant, though a bit awkward. Thirty minutes later, she showed up in line again with another child. This time, she didn't stumble, making it all the way up to me.

When her little companion climbed onto my lap, the woman bent over at the waist to talk to her. This time, I know, she was flashing Santa. It was quite obvious, as she looked directly at me and smugly smiled. I didn't know whether to put her on the naughty list or the nice list. So, I put her on both.

She kept her conversation going with the little girl for quite some time, offering nice, extended viewings. I kept up my end of the conversation, as it was a pleasant view. But, as with all nice views, they come and go.

When they stood up to leave, I wished the little girl well. She leapt off the stage and skipped back into the party. Then, I looked up at the cougar, grinned, and said, "Thank you."

She coyly smiled back and softly replied, "You're welcome, Santa. Merry Christmas." Even after this second encounter, no one else in the room realized what had gone on. Several minutes later, I could see her flowing mane, as she strutted out to her sports car and zoomed off into the day.

Easy come, easy go. I sit on the throne.

The evening's gig was a swinging, gigantic Christmas bash for a young, hip, and happening company. Spearheaded by a young, hip, happening couple (husband and wife), the venue had large searchlights shooting beams into the night sky. Valets were parking cars. I was waved through to a back lot, where caterers were unloading trays of food and cases of liquor.

Fat & Funny

When I walked into the building to find my employer, the first thing I saw was, not my employer. The first thing I saw was, another Santa. He was just as surprised to see me, as I was to see him. Our eyes popped wide, but not for long. When the door was thrown open by our young, bill-footing hosts, it was plain to see that they had started their party hours ago.

Our gulp of confusion is quickly dispelled, when the two of them, let the two of us know there wasn't a problem. The wife, who was the more hammered spouse, shouted, "Who gives a rat's ass?" Then, she started writing checks. Hubby accompanied her wild cackles with another deep swig from his tumbler of scotch. We quietly look on.

Then, the whirling dervishes spin on their heels and dash out the door to greet their arriving guests. Both startled Santas could only look at each other, shrug our shoulders, stash our checks, and continue changing.

When the time came for the party to start, the room was breathtaking—an over-the-top winter wonderland. After all, the place was a funky art space. It was quite funky *and* it was quite arty. With such elaborate decorations, it was apparent that our drunken hosts had been writing elaborate checks—and lots of them.

There were three bars, manned by fleets of bartenders. A disc jockey hovered over the proceedings, playing holiday music. Tuxedoed waiters strolled through the room with trays of appetizers and champagne.

When Santa One and Santa Too walked out onto the floor, one of the more sober assistants walked up, smiled, and took us aside. She explained, "Chase and Chelsea are so crazy. It's perfectly fine that the two of you are here. Why don't one of you stay close to the photo booth? The other one can just mingle with the guests. Trade places, whenever you want. Just play it by ear and have fun."

No problem, my dear, I thought. Our checks were already in our pockets.

The fun began. The first guests begin to arrive. I offered my fellow Santa the photo post. He sat, as I strolled out to the front door to greet folks. At this early hour, the elders arrived, nattily dressed in classy blazers and classier gowns. Appearing as if they'd just come from a gourmet dinner, they reeked of old money and looked like classic scenes from an old movie.

The music was mellow. Weak cocktails were served. I had learned about the 'weak cocktail theory' many moons ago.

Let me take a moment to flash back to my adolescence, my folks' crazy parties, and the words of my father. "When you're the host, pace yourselves," he would advise. "The first few drinks shouldn't be so ass-kicking strong. Ease into things. You don't want everyone passing out, in the first hour. You want your party to last, don't you?"

It was easy to see that these early arrivers were the wiser ones, the elders, the parents, and, most importantly, the big, big, big 'bill footers'. The men looked like Johnny Carson. Their wives looked like Angie Dickinson.

Sophistication permeated the event. This would not last long. Everyone was on their best behavior. This, also, would not last.

After twenty minutes, Santa One relieves Santa Too. As he headed off into the throes of the party, I perched myself on the throne. Directly beside me, sat a long table filled with silly hats, silly sunglasses, silly elf ears, silly antlers, and frilly red boas—a virtual Parrot Head paradise.

Fat & Funny

Ten feet directly in front of my throne, sat a professional photographer with lights and camera, action-ready. Our little area was quite festive and very well lit.

Those walking up to get their pictures taken were soft-spoken, polite, and respectful of Santa. We all realized we were about the same age, which came up in conversation. The photos were pleasant and swift. This, also won't last.

After the first hour, I could almost see the tide turn. As the older folk began to gather their coats, the younger folk began to show up, fashionably late.

The music began to crank up. The bartenders began pouring stronger drinks. Dean Martin and Frank Sinatra were replaced by Michael Jackson and Prince on the sound system. The party hits a higher gear, and a much higher decibel level.

At this point of the festivities, the weak cocktail theory goes right out the window. The younger folk jumped onto the disco floor. Though everyone was well dressed, the guys started letting their shirttails fly, and the girls started letting their mascara run.

By the third hour, the PA was at full blast. As Santa One and Too continued to walk around, trade places, and look at our watches, things started swerving sideways. By this time, our drunken hosts were completely, completely blitzed. So were their friends and coworkers.

Cue AASS # 2.

As I sat on my perch and midnight neared, it was apparent that Misty, a young executive with the company, wanted her picture taken with Santa. It was also apparent that Misty was sloshed. She visited the table and chose a tasteless set of oversized, purple sunglasses.

With a cocktail in one hand and a cigarette in the other, she stumbled on her heels toward me. As she settled onto my knee, she saw one of her friends. With a shrill, "Mallory! Oh, my God! Come here and take your picture with me and Santa," another young woman began to navigate her way onto my lap.

Mallory, who was just as snockered as Misty, plopped down on my other knee with her cocktail and cigarette, precariously perched above my red velvet (and probably flammable) suit. My first thought was, *Please don't spill anything on my suit, and please don't burn it with those stupid, fucking cigarettes.*

All night, the photographer had been instructing folks, "I'm going to count down from three, two, one, and we'll take the shot. Ready? Here we go." We all looked into the camera.

When the photographer said, "Smile," everyone smiled.

When the photographer said, "Three, two," we three, two-ed.

When the photographer said, "Damn it. There's something wrong with my camera. Hold on a minute," we held on a minute.

At this point, Mallory and Misty could no longer hold on a minute, leaning into each other with a kiss, followed by another kiss, and then a long, even-deeper kiss.

As the photographer continued fixing his camera, these two young girls continued to make out on my lap, as if I weren't even there. They paid absolutely no attention to me. I couldn't believe my eyes.

There I was, dressed up like Santa Claus, with two, young women, making out with each other on my lap. I could only silently chuckle to myself at the absurdity of it all.

After a bit, the photographer looked up and said, "Okay. Now I'm ready. Here we go. Smile. Three, two, one." Mallory and Misty unlocked lips and smiled. When they walked away, the photographer leaned over and asked, "Did I just see, what I think I just saw?" We both shook our heads and laughed.

The next folks walked up in a more traditional manner, and things returned to normal. The party continued. There was no further trace of either Misty or Mallory. Both just disappeared into the night, never to be seen again.

By the third hour, the place had turned into a sloppy, drunken fraternity party. Ties were completely taken off. Sport coats were piled onto tables. Gown straps no longer held up party dresses. Hairdos fell, like the snow outside.

As the partygoers sailed off into drunken oblivion, I soberly sat and watched the proceedings. When Santa Too came by, we both sat and watched the events.

After a while, it became very apparent that neither Santa had much meeting and greeting left to do. All we really had to do was hang around and watch the clock trudge toward midnight.

By this time, Santa's novelty had definitely worn off. No one even acknowledged the two, old men. No one engaged us in conversation. No one shook our hands. The focus of the party had shifted to the dance floor, the thudding lights, the flowing alcohol, and the grab-ass in the shadows.

Don't get me wrong—everyone was nice. But the sophistication of that first hour was replaced with a very unsophisticated fourth. After a while, it wasn't even entertaining to watch. No one seemed to mind, or even notice, that neither one of their Santas were even trying to be jolly, anymore.

We looked at each other and silently rolled our eyes. Once again, we reminded each other, "We've already been paid."

As the clock neared the witching hour, the place started to empty. When it did, it emptied fast. When it became apparent that Santa's purpose had completely run its course, we went looking for our hosts, to bid them good night.

After five minutes of searching, it became obvious that they were nowhere to be found. By this time, almost everybody was gone, and the DJ played Bing Crosby's "White Christmas." We looked at each other, shrugged our shoulders, headed to the dressing room, put our Santa suits back in their suitcases, shook hands, and headed into the December night.

With a two-hour gig that morning, and a four-hour gig that evening, I was dragging, to just get my head to the pillow—with visions of titties and tongues in my head.

A well-paying, double AASS day.

15

Santa goes to Christian College

Sometimes, religion will enter your Santa sphere. It's only natural, given the time of year. Sometimes, the two can be uncomfortable roommates. After all, they are eternally entwined. There's no getting away from each other. Santa appears around Christmas time and, strangely enough, flies around the world on Jesus's birthday.

What do the holidays mean to most modern people? Not much more than parties, commercialism, parties, shopping, drinking, eating, Black Friday, and on and on.

It's the time of the year to head up into the attic and bring down those large, wooden reindeer and that inflatable Santa. Illuminated plastic manger scenes are stuck out into front yards.

Dust them off. Light them up. Display them, loudly. *Gaudy* lawn scenes may say quite a bit about where you land in this disparate world.

Let the soiree begin.

One particular Christmas party was at a small, local Christian college. I had been hired for a late, Friday afternoon tree-lighting ceremony (after all the classes had finished for the semester). These gigs are easy peasy—just mingle and jingle and goof for the cameras.

Because I always like to make early contact, I called the dean's office several days in advance. I had been given the dean's number as my contact. His secretary informed me that he was busy at the moment, but she would gladly take my name and number.

The next morning, I received a call from a squeaky, young woman named Brittany, or Christie, or Tiffany. As we began to talk about the logistics of the gig, it felt like I was talking to my granddaughter.

So what? you say. The girl on the phone was a college student. My granddaughter is nine years old. Christie provided me with a polite greeting (ever-emotive) and information (which wasn't much).

When I hung up, I sighed to myself. Once again, I must realize that this is a young world, and I am old and in the way. But I've got a Santa Claus suit and I've got a gig at her college this Friday.

It was 3:45 when I showed up at their library for my 4:00 start. The campus was small, with a magnificent view of the city from its ivied perch on the hill. When I walked into the library, I learned that the ceremonies had been delayed until 4:30.

Thank goodness for crossword puzzles (another essential item for your suitcase). I was shown to a vacant office, and slowly began the transformation process. Within minutes, Tiffany knocked on the door. Her face was as cherubic and soft in person, as her voice was cherubic and loud on the phone. She was a wonderful person—just overly friendly, overly emotive, and really, really, really young.

She handed me an unmarked envelope with my fee, in cash— no receipt, no signatures, no nothing. Directly into my pocket that envelope went. Cash, eh? Cash is king in Santa World. We all know, cash is king in Jesus World, too.

Then, I had thirty minutes to wait. So, I wandered through the library and bought a bottle of water at the concession stand. Strewn all around, are lounging students, deep in thought and deep online.

At 4:15, Angela knocked again. When she asked if I could just go ahead and get started, it only took me a couple minutes to put on the coat and hat. This time, when I walked through the library, as Santa, some looked up, amused. Most just snickered and turned back to their tweeting phones. Once again, old and in the way.

When I walked out the door and onto the lawn, folks were starting to assemble. It was a lovely evening. Under a gigantic oak tree, a small, brass quartet played "Jingle Bells," "Silver Bells," "Here Comes the Sun", and "Here Comes Santa Claus." When I heard my song, I burst right into the throes of the party and started dancing around like Shemp Howard.

The faculty huddled off to the side, every member in a different shade of khaki and corduroy, with watches and jewelry to match. As the students started walking up, they arrived as a herd of Chads, with their Brittanys on their arms.

It was easy to see, this was a wealthy school. The children were all above average and Prairie Home Companioned. Their hair was neatly combed, their cheeks a healthy pink.

The band played on. When they did their rousing rendition of "Grandma Got Runned Over by a Reindeer," I walked right out in front of the band. In my best Marcel Marceau impersonation, I let everyone know that I don't like that song. I don't really dislike that song; it's just as stupid as any of my songs.

But my silly routine got a hearty laugh. The party continued. The evening sun began to set, crimson and orange, above the Nashville skyline.

Once again, some of the students smiled and engaged me. Many, though, turned and quickly walked off. Some completely ignored me. I tried to migrate to the merrier circles, where I found laughing children—I mean, college students.

It was a welcomed sight when I saw some laughing children—this time, actual children. When the kids of the faculty, and the grandkids of the financial pillars ran toward me, I took notice.

I politely excused myself from the undergrads, telling them, "I must tend to the young ones." They all smiled, understanding.

Angie informed me that there was a couch on the porch for me, in case I wanted to talk to any of the littler kids. I waved them all over.

For me, this was a wonderful change of pace. I enjoy interacting with smiling, little children, more than I like interacting with smug, grown children.

When little kids climbed onto the couch with me, they got very healthy, extended visits. I let them ramble on and on. Their long visits meant less time I had to spend out on the lawn, mingling.

I don't think anyone even realized what I was doing—just stalling, watching the clock, and biding my time with some little people. Oh, yeah, and sitting on a couch.

One of the main attractions of a good holiday gathering is the big table of snacks and drinks. The catering budget for this wealthy school was embarrassingly paltry, with just cookies, punch, s'mores, and a fire pit.

At five o'clock, after a couple songs and hymns from a choral group, I found myself hanging out near the stage. While the president of the college stepped to the microphone, a hush fell over the proceedings. I stopped jingling my bell and yuckin' it up. I stepped to the side. All attention focused on his words.

After a prayer, he launched into his message about the holidays. I stepped farther off to the side. When he started into his "list of holiday blessings," I tried to slip off into the shadows.

None of that worked. As he pontificated, one of the things he specifically wanted to thank Jesus for was—you guessed it—Santa Claus. Every bowed head looked up, and all eyes glued right on me. I froze, in embarrassment.

I had absolutely no idea this was going to happen. I had no idea what to do. I stood there like a reindeer in the headlights. I guess I hadn't faded into the bushes quite far enough.

Although I do not see the connection between Santa Claus and Jesus, I forced a sheepish smile and nod. Being a professional, I kept my cool. Being a human, I kept my disgust to myself.

Thankfully, his ramblings went on and on and onto other topics. By this time, I made sure I was way, way, way in the back, back, back, well behind the bushes.

At dusk, the ceremony would come to an end with the countdown and the lighting of the tree. When the dean stepped back up to the microphone and counted down to one, he threw the switch and the structure lit.

That's right—I said "the structure." No, it was not a tree. It was nothing more than a dozen strands of lights reaching to the top of a twenty-foot tetherball pole. (It seemed that the decoration budget matched the catering budget.) Still, the *oohs* and *ahhs* were audible.

With a new source of light thrown onto the lawn, the party

continued. I strolled toward the faculty gaggle. They were quite friendly. They were also quite ready to get gone and get home. In a matter of the next fifteen minutes, the place emptied of everyone over the age of twenty-two.

I once again found the couch and a couple more kids to visit with. After some funny conversations, I looked up to see the bustling lawn, completely devoid of people.

Two small groups of students, drinking punch and making s'mores, admitted, "Hey, Santa. The party's over."

As the holiday tetherball pole twinkled, a few stragglers walked through the light strands. When I sauntered over, they were admiring the conical shape and bidding each other adieu. When they left, no one remained.

I couldn't find any trace of Tiffany, or Brittany, or Christie, or Chad. The scheduled end of the party was still forty-five minutes away. I have said this many times: "I'm a hillbilly, but I'm not a stupid hillbilly." It was time for me to cut class.

As I strolled back toward the library, I was approached by a trio of young hippies. The two guys had beards, and the girl wore a nose ring and a stocking cap, resembling one of the seven dwarves. By their skunky aroma, it was easy to tell what they had been up to. Yay—someone I could relate to, instead of the Young Republican Caucus I'd been socializing with all evening.

All three wore stoned smiles. I could tell. I flashed back to 1969 and my college days, when I liked to get high and just participate in things. These folks were giggling and having a great time. After a few minutes though, I just found myself talking to some more young Caucasians. A lad with curly hair and a fledgling red beard asked, "I like kids. How can I get a job being Santa Claus?"

Fat & Funny

Once again, generation gaps emerged. When I gave my simple, obvious answer —"You just have to wait forty years, for your beard to turn white"—they all shook their heads and said, "Ooh. Wow. Yeah. Cool. Far out." I'm not sure they even realized that you must be old and have a white beard to be Santa.

Can I take comfort in teaching them some common sense, or should I have just shaken my head and walked away? I guess I did a little of both. I'm still not sure if anything I said, sunk in.

Anyway, the lawn was quiet. The fire in the pit was reducing to embers. I strolled back toward the library where one, final student on a bike stopped and asked for a quick photo. I smiled, wished her a merry Christmas, and walked into the building. As she rode off, the campus was eerily empty.

There, the subdued hush of the inside, replaced the quiet night of the outside. I looked at the clock on the wall and saw the party still had thirty minutes to go. Then, I looked around and found absolutely no sign of Angie, or Tiffany, or Chad, or Christie, or anyone. I quietly stepped back into my room and, in a few, short minutes, was undressed and ready to leave, suitcase in hand.

I don't like shortchanging folks. But this party just wasn't happening and I had been paid well—in cash. As I drove off campus, I looked back at the incubator that lay behind those ivied walls. For some odd reason, I didn't feel the least bit guilty about getting paid, handsomely.

Thank you, Jesus. Thank you, Lord.

16

Santa Hits the Gridiron

One gig was really fun. Santa hit the big time, making network TV. Believe me, the NFL and the Tennessee Titans are finely tuned machines and run a *very* tight ship. This gig was at Nissan Stadium, before 72,419 people.

For the few weeks leading up to it, I received daily e-mails, instructing me on exactly where I am allowed to go, exactly where I'm *not* allowed to go, and exactly when I'm supposed to be where I'm supposed to be. This is no problem, but it is a departure from my typical, "If you just want to show up a little before noon, you should be fine. The kids will get there a little after that."

Because the Titans' stadium is right downtown, it was easy for me to stop by on a quiet Thursday morning, meet the staff, and get my credentials and parking pass (thus, avoiding any kind of problems on football day). I was shown where I could dress—one of the smaller, spare locker rooms, which goes unoccupied on Sundays.

I was greeted by the director of cheerleaders, who was in charge of the mascots (I would be interacting with) and the flow of the pregame activities (I would be part of). When I assured her that I know how to become 'just another member of the cast', she smiled and breathed easy.

Fat & Funny

Sometimes, Santas can be cantankerous old men, but she and I hit it off well. She was completely professional and efficient about her gig, the same attitudes I take toward mine. She laid out a rough timeline for the pregame activities, which were scripted down to the minute.

I have no problem reading scripts. After appearing at a myriad of schools, malls, living rooms, and day-care centers, I had been looking forward to one of these highly-organized, high-profile gigs.

The NFL is the model of efficiency. The NFL on CBS runs like clockwork—literally, clockwork. Although I looked forward to being part of the cast, I realized that Santa would probably get a little more camera time than the rest.

When Sunday rolled around, I knew exactly where to go. I drove right onto the parking lot. When I flashed the correct credentials, I was waved right through rows and rows of barriers and orange cones, that were everywhere.

There wasn't much traffic at eight thirty in the morning. The folks who were already there were quietly stirring, milling around their campers, eating, drinking, and getting ready to take their tailgate parties into the stadium by noon.

When I walked up to the security gate, at nine in the morning, it was quiet—very quiet. There was no one in line, because there *was* no line. Later, there would be long, long lines. But at that time of the morning, I walked right up and right in.

Of course, the startled security officers wanted to know what I had in my green suitcase. When I told them, "I've got Santa Claus in there," guffaws echoed through the empty concourse. I threw in a hearty "Ho, ho, ho!" and strolled right through the gate.

I was escorted into the bowels of the stadium and into my locker room. There, I would suit up and prepare for the game, just as the players were doing down the hall and the cheerleaders were doing up the hall.

When I walked through the door, the smell of sweat and Bengay permeated the air. I had no problem with this. I've always liked the smell of sweat and Bengay. I also like the smell of incense and peppermints.

My initial thought was, *Oh, boy. This is really going to be fun.*

The team had asked that I be ready at 10:00. No problem.

At 9:19, the transformation began. At 9:36, I was big and red and jolly.

At 9:45, an office assistant showed up, to serve as Santa's chaperone for the day. She knew her way around the stadium very well. While she clutched her clipboard, with the script for the morning, I just followed along and went where I was told.

At 9:55, I made sure my cheeks were rosy, my breath smelled like a candy cane, and my beard was fluffy. I carried a single jingle bell at my side. It created a lovely tune.

On this game day, the stadium turnstiles opened at 10:00. At 9:59, I suddenly appeared, to welcome fans of both teams, as they streamed in. Everyone was in a festive holiday and football mood. Merriment exploded everywhere. The NFL was in the air.

I was instructed to just hang around, greet fans, and make merry. I already knew how to do that, quite well. By 10:01, I was doing that, quite well. I saw the relief in my chaperone's eyes.

At 10:20, I was led around to the turnstiles on the other side of the stadium. There, I burst onto the scene and did exactly what I was doing, back at the other gate (shaking hands, slapping backs, and taking pictures on a *lovely* Sunday).

Fat & Funny

All the while, I jangled my jingle bell for the kids. It's a subtle sound. Most adults don't even pay any attention. Children hear it, though. Anytime I see kids, my whole ballgame changes.

Of course, the adults wanted their pictures taken with Santa. Some were loud and pushy. Some were wearing silly outfits, and some were already well on their way to tipsy. All comers were obliged. But when I saw children, the adults were politely ignored. No one minds, when Santa needs to buddy up to some little buddies.

At 10:45, I was led upstairs, into one of the large open-air restaurants (for those fans, who want to pay a little extra for a buffet and Bloody Mary bar). A massive Christmas tree dwarfed the room. As I stationed myself at its base, dozens of fans approached with cameras. Everyone wore a smile and walked away with a bigger smile. I love this job.

At 11:00, I strolled over to a professional photographer with a long line of fans, all waiting for their picture in front of a Titans backdrop. When groups walked up, they were asked if they wanted Santa to be in their photo. If so, I ducked right into the frame, grabbed everyone by the waist, and drew them close for a nice, tight shot.

Some did not want Santa in their shot. This wasn't a big deal to me. I had absolutely no problem, spinning around and walking off into different spheres. But I found the attitude that some of the adults showed toward Santa to be a bit disheartening. Several of them, who didn't want Santa in their shot, *really* didn't want Santa in their shot. Some showed downright disgust with the whole notion of Santa Claus. If looks could kill. But like I said, I have no problem walking away. As you know, I'm not a big Christmas guy, but a few of these fans had really bad attitudes. I just wanted to say, "And a lump of coal in your stocking, may I bring?"

At 11:30, I was whisked into an elevator and escorted halfway down the tunnel to the field, where I was staged, purposely hidden from the fans. I was introduced to T-Rac, the Titan's mascot, who also had his game face on. Actually, it was a game *head*—a large, fuzzy head of a racoon, Tennessee's state animal. We both sported Santa hats.

I was reminded of the dog days of baseball in the 1980s, when I hung around Busch Stadium quite a bit with John Kendall, the St. Louis Cardinals' original Fredbird (both in and out of his costume). I used to love to watch him jump around on the field in that giant, foam head and those big, floppy feet. He was like watching a "One Stooges" routine. John was, and still is, an agile man. So is T-Rac. You must be nimble to be a mascot. Those big, floppy feet demand it.

As I stood in the shadows and watched the big scoreboard clock above the field, I was shown the exact timeline for the pregame festivities. Also readied at the mouth of the tunnel, was T-Rac's modified four-wheeler. Usually, his cart resembles a monster truck, but this day it had been transformed into a Santa mobile, decorated with red ribbons, garlands, and sprigs of pine.

He and I stepped onto the cart, and I found a solid handle to grip. He said he wouldn't drive too crazy and that we were just going to take a couple loping laps around the field.

When the PA announcer bellowed, "Ladies and gentlemen, please direct your attention to the north end zone and welcome Teeee-Raaaac!" the roar of the crowd was thunderous. When the announcer continued with "And it appears as if he has a special friend with him!" the roar of the seventy thousand people was breathtaking.

T-Rac gave it a little gas and we lunged forward onto the playing field. I had no trouble with balance. He was a very smooth and considerate driver. As we cruised around the field, I waved to the crowd, which was cheering like crazy. It was quite surreal.

After the first lap, he leaned over and asked if we should make another one. When I yelled, "Hit it!" we rode out onto the logo at midfield and took a couple more spins around it.

The whole episode took only a few minutes (11:37–11:42, to be exact). When we got back to where we started, at the bottom of the ramp, he slowed down. As I hopped off the cart and began to stroll around the end zone, he headed back up the tunnel. I immediately started waving to the crowd and dancing around like Chubby Checker.

Network cameras were everywhere, waiting for the teams to emerge from that same tunnel. Santa mugged for all of them. Later that evening, friends who knew about my gig, called to say they had seen me on their network feed. They also told me, how silly I looked. All I did was goof around and act like Dick Van Dyke.

When I looked back up the ramp, I saw the massive Denver Broncos stomping down, shoulder to shoulder, tattoos ablaze, nostrils flared, anxious to hit the field and anything that got in their way. Believe me, I jumped *way* out of their way. I let that stampede roar right past.

After the Broncos were on the field, the Titans emerged from their tunnel, running through billows of smoke and fire. While the explosions resembled a Kiss concert, I dashed back out into the end zone and danced around like Curly Howard.

With both teams on the field, the refs gathered and the fans settled into their seats. I was told to just hang out in the end zone and keep on keeping on. When the cheerleaders started to congregate in their skimpy red uniforms, Santa walked right up and started dancing with them.

Now, tell me—who wouldn't want to dance with Santa Claus? But, just like some of the sulkier fans earlier, some of the cheerleaders didn't want anything to do with me. Others smiled, showing their dazzling white teeth. We immediately started jitterbugging.

When the scoreboard clock began to count down the final few minutes before kick-off, attention shifted from the sideline to the gridiron. I was ushered off the field, back up the ramp, into an elevator, and up to several luxury boxes overlooking the field. I stomped right in, with a cheerleader on each arm.

The view from these suites, high over the fifty-yard line, is just that—sweet. I had to stop in my tracks and watch a couple plays. This was no big deal. Most of the guys wanted their pictures taken with the cheerleaders, anyway.

A few wanted to hang with the old, fat guy, but most of the attention was definitely given to those statuesque women. When children were in the suite, I played with them. They didn't have much interest in the cheerleaders, either.

After a few minutes, we were led from Suite 233 to Suite 236. Then, it was up another elevator to Suites 333, 334, and 335, which were even larger and contained wealthier season-ticket holders. The catering spreads were spectacular. Alcohol flowed freely. My chaperone continued to clutch her clipboard, with her list of suites that had requested a visit from me and my leggy elves.

Then, we went right back down to the field for the second quarter. I helped with a couple on-field promotions, that took place during one of the many television time-outs.

I was handed one of those enlarged, Ed McMahon-sized checks and instructed to walk it right out to the middle of the end zone. A contestant was blindfolded under the goalpost. If she could grope around and find her way to the check in my hand, she would be the grand-prize winner. She had thirty seconds.

As I walked out, the corporate regional assistant district manager, who had handed me the check, whispered, "Try not to make it too obvious." We both chuckled, as he slapped me on the back. When our contestant was led onto the field, the crowd started going nuts, screaming "Turn left!" and "Turn right!"

I kept my eyes on the clock directly over my right shoulder, as well as the teams on the field, huddled directly over my left shoulder. As she waved her hands in front of her, I nonchalantly strolled nearby.

The clock wound down and the crowd rose up. Right before time expired, I let her grab the check. The crowd cheered. When she threw off her blindfold and jumped into the air, I stepped out of the picture.

She was interviewed. She was the winner. She was on camera. I was already off to my next assignment. Of course, when the camera turned to me, I mugged with a silly Pee-wee Herman dance. Everyone could see my muggings on the Jumbotron.

The referee blew his whistle. Play on the field resumed. Those players are massive. While we bided our time on the sideline, waiting for the next promotional time-out, a long, spiraling pass and three speeding football players thundered our way. Although they didn't bulldoze us, they did come fairly close, literally shaking the ground we stood upon.

There were a couple more spots, another contest, and a plethora of photo ops, all culminating with the cheerleaders' on-field dance routine to "Jingle Bell Rock." As the second quarter began to wind down, they formed a chorus line across the Titans logo in the middle of the field. I was instructed to just hang out on the shoulder and jingle bell rock along.

When Bobby Helms began to blare from the PA system, I started doing a little jig, aimed more for the kids, who were probably watching me. Once again, I knew the adults were focused on the posings of the cheerleaders. I inconspicuously did a little dance on the sidelines and waved to the little kids—while acting like a big kid.

As play resumed, the cheerleaders all ran off the field together, excitedly gathering around me. Smiles and cameras flashed, as Santa crashed their cheerleader party. As halftime neared, they scattered to the four corners of the field.

When halftime arrived and all the players headed to their respective locker rooms, it got fairly quiet on the field. My gig was almost over. The PA announcer bellowed, "And let's hear it one more time, for Santa Claus. Byyyye, Santa!" I made a final dash out into the end zone and gave a final wave to the crowd. Then, I disappeared into the tunnel and was gone—to another, late-afternoon gig across town.

Although I had been hired to be there until 2:30, no one seemed to mind my leaving, explaining, "The first half of the game is about dancing and mascots and promotions. The second half is about football."

There were to be no more contests for me, no more dance routines, and no more sleigh rides. I was handed my check and headed off to my locker room, to get dressed as quickly as I could. Then, I left for the parking lot as quickly as I could, well before any possible hint of a traffic jam.

As I strolled out to my truck, over my shoulder, I could hear the roar of the crowd and the start of the second half. The public address announcer bellowed again and again and again.

I calmly drove from the stadium and on to my next gig. I tuned my radio to the game and listened to the second-half action, chuckling to myself.

A YouTube clip of my Jingle Bell Rock rendition can be found at **https://www.youtube.com/watch?v=euC6ONze0ws**.

It was a wonderful way to spend a Sunday. The sky was a brilliant blue.

17

Not Every Moment Is Golden

Not every moment of every gig is going to be filled with visions of sugarplums, dancing in your head. Occasionally, smack-dab in the middle of all the rejoicing, depression and ugly will rear its ugly head.

Emotions are high this time of year. Situations can be tense. I sit on my perch and see it all. Sometimes, it's not a pleasant sight.

One little girl walked up, but didn't have much of a smile. Her dress was a bit ruffled, though her hair was nicely combed, gently held back with reindeer barrettes. Her brothers and cousins were very excited and very rowdy. Her, not so much. The family all walked up together.

After the initial outbursts of, "Hey, Santa, I want a bike" died down, I began to quietly take them in, one by one. This way, I could give each of them some comfort and, more importantly, a chance to confide.

I made sure I talked to her, last. After each brother and cousin jumped from my lap and clambered off, I helped her climb up. I could tell this was not going to be a bowl of cherries.

I began slowly. With each question, she gnashed on her knuckles and mumbled through her fingers. I literally had to, ever so gently, lower her hands, just so I could hear her voice. She was not a chatty Cathy.

My chatty questions were easy: "Do you have a tree? Is it beautiful? Are you ready for Christmas?"

Her unchatty answers were just as easy: "Yes. Yes. Yes."

After a handful of softballs, I got down to business. I hit her with the big one: "What would you like for Christmas?"

(*Santa tip 3b:* Santa should always ask, "What would you like?" instead of "What do you want?" "What do you want?" can sound so brash. Sometimes, it can come out, sounding not so nice. The child may have just heard Uncle Roger yell, "What do you want?" at Aunt Ethel. His, "What do you want?" may not have been delivered with the nicest of tone, or civility. It's much nicer and a whole lot softer to ask, "What would you like?")

So, I asked her, "What would you like for Christmas?"

Then, the sniffling started. Then, tears began. I drew her close and whispered my question again. Then, she sobbed, "I want my mommy and daddy to stop fighting and not get divorced anymore."

Folks, this is a rough one. When this happens (and occasionally, it will), it is everything I can do, to keep from tearing up.

Others cry, "I want my grandpa to stop drinking."

Some say, "I want my grandma to not have cancer."

Others beg, "I want my sister to stop hitting me," and some cry, "I want my dad to come home from the army."

You get the picture.

Sometimes, this is very hard to take. Once again, you'll feel futile and absolutely helpless. Feelings flutter.

I don't completely dismiss their pleas, but I do my best to

quickly move on. I try to convey, "Don't worry, little sweetie. Things will all work out. Christmas is almost here. Do you like pizza?" Hopefully, another diversionary question or two will pull the train back up onto the tracks. Then, I can resume with sugarplums and candy canes.

Like I said in the introduction of this book, I am not a fan of Christmas. I understand thoroughly, the depression and loneliness people can feel in the middle of a festive, holiday crowd. I've felt it many, many times. I feel it every December. I've just learned how to live with it. I will admit that, at times, I still get overtaken with melancholy. I know what to do. I know what helps snap me out of it. No, I'm not going to recommend tequila, though it does work for me.

Some of the saddest things I have ever heard, have come from the mouths of children. As Santa, there are three, surefire ways to buck up and move on. It's easy: 1) get back to business, 2) get back to your gig, and 3) move on to the next child.

It's heartbreaking.

Children aren't the only ones affected.

One Christmas party was running swell—6:00 to 7:30 on a crisp, chilly, Friday evening. Early hours, happy hour, happy people, easy gig.

With the party held in the clubhouse of a terraced neighborhood, everyone "in the hood" knew they could conveniently stop by with their kids, directly after work, have some punch, and get a photo with Santa. This early time slot would still give them latitude to make it home, rearrange the children, rearrange themselves, and make it back out the door, for a night on the town. It was a great idea.

The evening started as fine as fur. Christmas lights sparkled—there were hundreds of them. Christmas carols sprayed from the speakers in the ceiling. The children were boisterous, but behaved. They'd just had a long, grueling week of first grade and were ready for the weekend. Although they were still wound tight, they were considerate and well mannered. We were having a ball.

I could see my hostess / employer flitting about the room, making sure everyone was having a jolly time. She had extended the same hospitality to me over the phone the previous week (in our pre-gig conversation) and earlier in the evening, when I had arrived (before Santa made his entrance). In a nutshell, she was a lovely and very pleasant human.

She had decorated the room, herself. She had decorated herself, herself. She had baked the cookies, herself. By herself, she was making sure no one wanted for anything.

Her smile lit up the back of the room. I could see her wrist-jingling friends, from my armchair by the tree. Not only was she having a party; I could tell she was having a blast.

Her two boys (ages three and five) were also in the feistiest of festive moods. They frantically ran around the room with their friends, ate cookies, drank juice boxes, and hopped about, like sugared-up kids do.

She, as well as her well-heeled friends, jangled their jewelry, sipped their white wine, checked their cell phones, checked their lipstick, and watched their children revel in holiday spirit.

I didn't sip any wine. I didn't jangle any jewelry. I'm always glad to bring spirit. Santa doesn't carry a cell phone.

It was an easy gig for me—ninety minutes of mayhem,

flashbulbs, and shtick. The children laughed and shrieked and played. The din was palpable. Things were proceeding nicely.

Then, I could see them begin to proceed not so nicely. I could see the beginnings of a commotion in the far back corner of the room.

Then, I saw him walk in, sporting stubble, tan overalls and a hunting cap. Although his boys raced to greet him, I could tell he wasn't in any kind of Christmas mood. I could see the color flush from her face. I could see her friends stationed nearby. It was very uneasy to see.

I couldn't hear what was being said, but I could easily tell, things were not warm and fuzzy. Voices weren't raised. It didn't get loud. But I could tell, things really were not well.

No one else in the party could really see the potential powder keg in the back of the room. But from where I sat, I had a bird's-eye view. There was nothing I could do to help diffuse the situation. I had a gaggle of children at my feet and several more waiting in line.

I saw him and my hostess step outside. As they did, her girlfriends huddled into 'gossip formation', before returning to 'party mode'. Then, our hostess stepped back into the room—alone.

When she walked back in, she motioned to her boys, grabbed their coats, gathered them in her arms, and whispered to them. When the boys heard the news, they started quietly sobbing. They *really* wanted to stay at the party.

But it was obvious, that was not going to happen. It was also obvious what was going on. They all stepped out into the night, together.

Michael Supe Granda

The party carried on. Children continued to tell me what they wanted for Christmas. It was business as usual, for me.

Ten minutes later, our hostess stepped back into the room. Tears filled her eyes, as her girlfriends huddled around, helping her gather her composure and fix her mascara.

Sheepishly, she reentered the party with a deflated, reddened smile.

While all of this was taking place, Santa was still in full swing. The little kids were still gathered around. They handed me wish lists and I handed them candy canes. They were still in holiday mode. I was still in cartoon land.

It wasn't long before everyone started to migrate toward the door. Everyone had a cookie and some punch. Everyone had their picture taken. Off into the night, they all skipped.

As quickly as the room had filled at 6:00, it began to empty at 7:20. One by one, the hostess hugged her guests. Mustering all the courage she could, she smiled, bidding everyone muffled adieus.

By 7:40, the room had completely emptied, except for me, her, and a couple of her friends, who had stayed behind to help clean up the place. (The mess wasn't terribly bad. Paper cups, paper plates, plastic forks, and cookie crumbs—that's about it. These gals weren't going to be breaking any nails).

She sighed, as she handed me my check. I could tell her evening had been badly bruised. I had worked her party for several years, and we had become friends. She looked at me with moist eyes. It was all I could do, to keep mine dry.

She thanked me several times, then fell into a warm, Santa bear hug—the same kind of embrace I give to the children, who need or want one. When I looked at her, I tried to convey calm and empathy.

As I gathered my things and headed for the door, I really felt badly for her. I was done. I was headed home. She still had an empty room and a couple of her friends by her side. The clean-up continued.

When I stepped outside and clomped up to my darkened truck, over my shoulder, I could still see the brightly lit windows and the tree with the sparkling lights and the fireplace and the wreath on the door.

I could also see her in the window, sobbing onto the shoulders of her friends. It appeared as if they were headed for an Oprah moment and a Dr. Phil remedy, all courtesy of Ernest and Julio Gallo. It was a somber way to end a joyous evening.

I got to the truck, undressed, hopped in, and warmed it up. When the dome light went off and I was ready to leave, I looked back to the lit clubhouse. All the lights were still on, but I knew the heartbreak and sorrow that remained inside.

Happy not-so-merry Christmas. I understand the sorrow.

Hopefully, next year, she and her ex will not be as contentious.

Not every moment is golden.

18
Pirates, Ornaments, and Garbonzos

Being musical isn't necessary to be Santa. I just happen to be. Music has consumed my life since I was twelve, learning how to play "Love Me Do" and "Lucille." To this day, playing music keeps me young at heart. Every time I pick up my guitar, I turn into a teenager, trying to pick the dickens out of "Johnny B. Goode."

This musical gift is a blessing. It's had a wonderful presence in my 'non-Santa' life, as well. It has taken me around the world, onto the silver screen, onto the boob tube, into recording studios, onto stages under full moons, into caves and parades, and far out into left field. All of this, I've done alongside some of my favorite people.

A few of my favorite, left-field endeavors are ... hmm. Let me think for a minute .... (Let's all scratch our chins and fade out of focus.)

(Fade in)

Tom Mason and I have been friends, actors, bandmates, and cowriters for decades. A brilliant guitarist and primitive trombonist, he has been a mainstay in my many versions of Supe and the Sandwiches. Some folks call us song-and-dance men, which is fine with us. Every gig we've ever played has involved nothing short of silly song and hilarious dance.

We've shared the screen, both with acting roles in independent films: *Blazers and Blackbirds* and *The Atomic Ape*. Both flicks had very low budgets, but were two tons of fun. Although Tom and I gave award-winning performances (wink, wink), neither movie garnered any kind of acclaim or attention.

Not only have we played gigs; we've written songs together. Our writing sessions resemble our gigs, as silly as a barrel of monkeys. One of our first collaborations was a tune, entitled, "Yo, Ho, Ho (Pirate's Christmas)".

Tom and I found the irony and phonics of "yo, ho, ho" and "ho, ho, ho" too fertile to pass up. He transformed into Red Beard, while I morphed into Kringle. We picked up our guitars and got after it.

As we wrote the song, we also had to write the story—a tale of Santa Claus, who has loaded too many toys onto his sleigh. As he struggles to navigate the foggy evening, he is approached by a pirate ship, whose captain has taken notice of Rudolph's nose.

Michael Supe Granda

When the crafts pull alongside each other, the two men meet. Santa pleads his case. The pirate volunteers his crew, who saves the day. They unload the sleigh and make sure all the gifts are distributed to the boys and girls around the world. St. Nick's peril is over.

He and the pirate become fast friends, sharing song, laughter, and tales of hot buttered rum. Then, Santa and his new compadres get tanked-up, filling with holiday cheer.

Off to sea, they shove. Christmas is saved. The children are happy. Ships ahoy. Hip, hip, hooray. Ho, ho, ho. Yo, ho, ho. So on and so on.

Fronting his band, the Blue Buccaneers, Tom travels the world, playing festivals and celebrating pirates and ships and oceans, oh my. He once observed, "We *have* to travel. There aren't many oceans around Nashville."

In complete regalia, the Blue Buccaneers storm their every stage. Their high-energy show often crescendos with Tom

Fat & Funny

playing his guitar while perched atop a chair, perched atop a table, or marching upon the length of the bar. As I have done with Santa, he has turned this into a resourceful, rent-paying endeavor. Ahh, the artist's life.

After writing "Pirate's Christmas," we had the bright idea of making a video for the song. He had a camera. Two heads are better than one. It was a perfect idea.

He went into his laundry room and set up a green screen in front of his washer and dryer. With all the window shades open and three bright lights, we were ready—a two-man film crew.

He donned full pirateness and I pulled my Santa suit out of mothballs. In our costumes, we just goofed around and lip-synched the song into the camera. Tom would later edit the footage and superimpose crazy scenes onto the green screen behind us. One of the funnier asides to this tale is, we filmed the song in the summer. It was hot and muggy in Tennessee.

We set up the camera angle and delivered four minutes of holiday mayhem—in the middle of August—directly under some hot lights. We felt like two patty melts, under the lamps at O'Charley's. When the director (one of us) yelled, "Cut!" it took four seconds to rip off our coats and dive toward his air-conditioner.

We only did two or three takes of the song. That was enough. We both agreed that we had more than enough goofy footage to fill out a goofy, four-minute video. Then, while the camera was still on, the lights were still focused, and I was still in my Santa suit, I pantomimed a version of my song, "I'm Gonna Be Santa Claus for Christmas." Tom would also edit this footage into another goofball video. It didn't take us long to reach absolute goofballogy.

We thought it would be funny if, over the course of the song,

I was to play every instrument he had in his house. We gathered them all around, as he sat on the floor at my feet, just beneath the camera frame. As the song played, one by one, he handed each instrument up to me, and I just clowned around with it.

The entire video was done in only one take. When we watched the playback, it was obvious there was no need for a second take. We both laughed so hard, we had to hold our sides. (Note to reader: This happens every time Tom and I see each other. We like laughing so hard and holding our sides.)

Then, we stuck our faces back into his air-conditioner. It was a very funny, very hot day.

On the finished videos, he replaced the green screen behind us with stock footage from a couple obscure movies. I have no idea what they are.

1. "Yo, Ho, Ho" sported grainy footage of pirates, kegs of rum, sword fights, and raging storms in the night - from an old, swashbuckler flick.
2. "I'm Gonna Be Santa Claus" fronted a repeating twenty-second clip from some tacky, foreign Christmas film in my library.

Tom spliced my holiday clip into an endless loop behind me. Making absolutely no attempt at any kind of finesse or subtlety, it is very sunny and low-tech funny. While a sea of fake snow, candy canes, and elves danced behind me, I delivered my autobiographical lyrics about getting old and gray and dumpy.

The campy background fits perfectly with the campy song, sung by the campy guy playing a banjo, a trumpet, a trombone (both at the same time), and a sitar.

Fat & Funny

I'm Gonna Be Santa Claus for Christmas

I'm gonna be Santa Claus for Christmas. I've got everything I need
A beard so big and white, it glows in the night
And a big ol' belly. When I laugh, it shakes like a bowl of jelly
I've got some snow-white gloves and some coal-black boots
I'm gonna be Santa Claus for Christmas
I even bought me a Santa Claus suit

I stopped shaving in September and started eating everything in sight
It was doughnuts every morning and beer every night
By the middle of November, I looked like a rusty old can
But by the first of December, I looked like a jolly old man

I love to see the faces of the children as I leisurely walk by
In a pair of faded blue jeans, I see the twinkle in their eye
I love to hear them giggle, as they crinkle up their nose
I give them all a chuckle and a wiggle and a couple, "Ho, ho, hos"

Michael Supe Granda
Yo, Ho, Ho (A Pirate's Christmas)

'Twas, the night before Christmas and out on the sea
We were cold, lonely pirates. It was no place to be
We needed one more raid in the freezing rain
To make it to the warmth of the Spanish main

As we passed St. John's on Newfoundland's coast
A strange-looking frigate appeared like a ghost
The bowsprit was carved like an Arctic reindeer
With a lantern nose, to make their passage clear

> Yo ho ho—surrender the booty
> Yo ho ho—we're here to receive
> Yo ho ho—it's a pirate's Christmas
> And we're a pack of bloodthirsty thieves
> Argghhhh

We got along broadside and prepared to board
With bloodthirsty cries, we raised our swords
But we cast no fear on the curious crew
A strange pack of pygmies of a lighter hue

Out of the fo'c's'le, their captain appeared
He was a corpulent man, with a great white beard
He wore a suit of red with furry, white trim
He laughed in our faces, as we shouted at him

Fat & Funny

We said, "Yo ho ho. Surrender the booty"
He said, "Ho ho ho. Not on my dead man's chest
It's Christmas Eve and it's my duty
To get the toys to the children, who've been on their best"

There'd been such good behavior by all the girls and boys
That Santa's ship was sinking from the weight of all the toys
I looked in the deadlights of my befuddled crew
They'd faced lots of dangers, but this one was new

I offered the fat Spaniard our brigantine
To deliver his gifts clear to the Caribbean
I warned him, we traded in treachery
He said, "Ho ho ho. Your secret's safe with me"

Yo ho ho. Deliver the booty
Ho ho ho. Take my treasure chest
It's Christmas Eve and it's all our duty
To get to the children, who've been on their best

Yo ho ho. Merry Christmas
Ho ho ho and a hot, buttered rum
Yo ho ho. It's s pirate's Christmas
Yo ho ho. Hey, rum pa pum pum

Every December, the Blue Buccaneers play numerous holiday shows. When they do, I have an open invitation to their stage, to sing our song, which I adore. I will sit in the green room for an hour, as they run their show. But when "Yo, Ho, Ho" pops up on the song list, usually near the end of their set, I suit up, psych up, and burst onto the stage to deliver Santa's silly lines.

You can see "Yo, Ho, Ho (Pirate's Christmas)" on YouTube at **http://www.youtube.com/watch?v=WARx0LT_v6Q.**

You can see "I'm Gonna Be Santa Claus for Christmas" on YouTube at **https://www.youtube.com/watch?v=V7n-z1lSEJI.**

Both videos are a riot. Both videos are silly stories about our silly art projects.

Cecil B. DeMille would laugh his ass off.

(fade out)

(fade in)

Jen Gunderman is not only a professor of American music history for the Blair School of Music at Vanderbilt University, she is also a very talented and in-demand keyboardist and accordionist. She has toured for years with Sheryl Crow and the Jayhawks, and spent many evenings onstage with Supe and the Sandwiches, Mark & Mike, and the Garbonzos at East Nashville's legendary Family Wash.

A wonderfully creative soul, who works alongside bassist James "Hags" Haggerty (Blues Bros.) and drummer Martin Lynds (Grassy Knoll Boys), the three have carved out their own holiday tradition—the Ornaments.

Fat & Funny

The Ornaments play to sold-out crowds every year, performing Vince Guaraldi's "A Charlie Brown Christmas" in its entirety. The gig is reverent and refreshingly low volume. As smooth, jazz licks fly about the room, it is a welcome respite from the waves of Americana we surf in our daily, Nashville lives.

The trio appeals, not only to the kids in the crowd, but also to the adults, who still remember the role Guaraldi's masterpiece played in their younger lives. Now, they want to pass that feeling of warmth on to their children. We are all fond of the role Charlie Brown has played in our lives.

On occasion, the Ornaments will give Santa a call on his 'Bat Phone'. Their entire presentation lasts about forty-five minutes, which leaves them some extra time to fill out a longer show. This they deftly do with a handful of standards and holiday classics.

And what better way to fill some time than with Santa Claus dancing around onstage, acting like an idiot, and singing "Run, Run, Rudolph"?

Thus, Jen's phone call. Usually, my Santa is just a sedentary couch potato. But on this gig, Santa plays guitar, sings, and loves Chuck Berry. Looks like I'm three for three. Put me in, coach.

The Ornaments graciously let me sling on some rock 'n' roll and take a stab at my lame Duckwalk. It's a wonderful time and a wonderful sound, with a stand-up bass, drums, piano, saxophone, and me. Plus, everyone on that stage really knows how to "swing the sleigh."

The first thing most guitar players will do at a gig, is test out all the foot pedals that lay at their feet—or, as famed record producer, Lou Whitney would deem it, their "talent station." The next thing they do, is make sure their lead guitar volume is loud enough and distorted enough. The first and only thing I do, is make sure my guitar goes *plunkety, thunkety, twang.*

It's really rewarding to see children in the holiday spirit. They have just enjoyed a beautiful, uplifting show and are dancing with their grandpas. Others, hug and swing each other around, as if they were still out on their playground.

It's wonderful to see multiple generations *lettin' that rock 'n' roll get all up inside 'em*—led by this grandpa in his red suit.

I fit right in. Jen and the boys have perfected a very important musical skill—how to play rock 'n' roll, with proper emphasis on the roll. Many young musicians know how to rock. Sadly, too few pay attention to the role of the roll.

We're all fans of Little Richard, Fats Domino, and Chuck Berry. The Ornaments know how to Chuck Berry.

I quietly wait in the green room, half-dressed, guitar tuned, and ready to roll. Like my appearance with Tom's pirates, my slot with the Ornaments is at the end of the show. This means Santa has to wait for a long while in the dressing room for his brief shot in the spot.

Fat & Funny

Tom Petty said it best, when he wrote, "The waiting is the hardest part." But I've learned how to deal with the waiting. It's just a mindset. It's not musical at all. Most artists know how to slip into, and out of the waiting.

If you think it's hard to wait and wait and wait, it isn't. Just as long as you keep 'the show' in the forefront of your mind. A four-minute song is worth a forty-minute wait. Yes, folks, the thrill and the rush of that four minutes, is well worth it.

When Santa starts to shake it, the whole place shakes it. That's how Santa likes it. That's how Chuck likes it. That's how I like it. I love it, when everybody is just rollin' and tumblin' together.

Michael Supe Granda

Santa is a ham and a real crowd-pleaser, not only for the folks out in the audience, but for the folks up on stage. While the crowd rollicks in the aisles, the smiles on the bandstand make me realize, "We just might be doing a pretty good thing, here."

A clip of our 2021 appearance at Nashville's Eastside Bowl can be found on You Tube at **https://www.youtube.com/watch?v=2mYolNnznXQ.**

In January 2016, after another busy holiday season, I wanted to record a Christmas album, that would feature the litter of holiday songs I'd recently written. In the first week of January, I booked a recording studio (Fry Pharmacy) and gathered the Sandwiches (Jen, Tom, Mark Horn, and Scott McEwen).

Throughout December, we all had numerous gigs. We knew all the songs and were playing quite well. Before the holiday sheen had worn off, I wanted to capture it onto tape.

While everyone was still basking in the glow, I asked my bandmates to come to the session, dressed in their festive garb (that hadn't made it into the back of their closets yet). With instruments, spirit, decorations, libations, and food, we went into the studio. In a three-day span, we recorded "Cool, Cool, Yule" (Missouri Mule Music 000015).

Everyone thought it was a cool idea. Everyone showed up with bells on and played their asses off. We ate and drank and rolled and rocked and laughed. By the second week of January, we had a cool, cool Christmas record in the can.

"Cool, Cool, Yule" can be found at **www.supeline.com** and on CDBaby at www.cdbaby.com.

(fade out)

(fade in)

Last but definitely not least, we have the Garbonzos—my favorite of all my side projects. Fronted by accordion wizard, Chris Slatinsky and fiddler/washboardist, John "Indian" Ehlers, I met the Kansas City natives in the early seventies, while attending Southwest Missouri State College.

When the Garbonzos play, every gig is a combination of Mardi Gras, Christmas, Halloween, a drunken melee, and a six-year-old's birthday party.

I was already in a band. But when I saw the Garbonzos singing and playing polkas, while sloshing through the fountains of the college—accompanied by two guitar players, a trombonist, a juggler, and a guy banging two metal trash can lids as cymbals—I fell in love with the music.

And when I saw them running amok like the Marx Brothers, wearing completely absurd costumes like ballet tutus, Viking helmets, grass skirts, and duck decoys taped to their heads, I fell in love with the absurdity.

As they roamed through the crowd, adding festive ambience

to the scene, I recognized bohemian street theater, at its finest. I immediately asked if I could join the band, saying I could wear a Santa suit to any gig at any time of year, and fit right into the fray.

Not only does Chris know every polka, he also knows every holiday song and Christmas carol. Often, he will break into "Jingle Bells" or "The Twelve Days of Christmas" in the middle of July. No one ever seems to mind. Everyone sings along.

In the spring of 1972, I became a Garbonzo. My first gig was in the St. Patrick's Day parade, meandering through the streets of Springfield, Missouri, on a beautiful March day. I donned my most obnoxious pair of green pants, grabbed my mandolin, and headed to the parade site. There, I joined the majestic array of humanity. We were a full-blown tidal wave of *everything bizarre and green under the sun*.

This time, there were a handful of guitarists, two saxophones, a trombone, a clarinet, a couple drummers, and a bunch of green people playing kazoos, jangling tambourines, and dancing about.

As part of the SMS Independent Marching Band, our "float" simply consisted of the Garbonzos and thirty of their friends. We became an amoebic green mob, strolling through the streets of Springfield, playing "Louie, Louie," "Jingle Bells," "Tequila" and "The Beer Barrel Polka" over and over and over.

Since that day, I have been a proud, card-carrying member of the band. For the past fifty years, I've lived out every one of my Three Stooges, Spike Jones, Frank Zappa, Bonzo Dog Doo-Dah Band, and Monty Python fantasies, just by being a *Garbonzo*.

Fat & Funny

The sillier we acted, the more folks liked it. The sillier we acted, the greater the theatrics. The sillier we acted, the more they paid us.

There is a definite art form to the "business of ridiculous." I've studied it all my life. I learned early on, that the court jester is a legitimate occupation, that pays very well. Once again, I may be a hillbilly. I'm not a stupid hillbilly.

Along with long-time guitarist, Tim White, the four of us have traveled the world, as part of the Sister Cities' cultural exchange program. We've played festivals in Isesaki, Japan, and Tlaquepaque, Mexico (Springfield's Sister Cities). We felt honored to be in each city.

The Japanese went bonkers for us. They love their cartoons, so we drank sake and turned ourselves into human cartoons. They were the most gracious of hosts, and we were the most grateful of guests. A wonderful time was had by all.

Tlaquepaque is located in the tequila capital of Jalisco province. Oddly enough, tequila is the official drink of the Garbonzos. It turns us into cartoons, and I love being a cartoon. We are a match, made in agave heaven. I've always had a wonderful relationship with the stuff.

As we were performing on the festival's main stage, the mayor walked out, mid-set, with an open bottle of tequila in his hand. In the middle of a song, he started to pour it into our mouths. We couldn't say no. He was the mayor. You don't say no to the mayor. That would be rude. Another wonderful time was had by all.

Because of the acoustic nature of the band, electricity is not a requirement for a gig. This has taken us into parades, onto float trips, into full-moon solstices, onto riverbanks, into political arenas, and around campfires all over the world.

Over the decades, a Garbonzo specialty is the myriad of Christmas gigs they can play, sometimes as many as three and four a day. If needed, Santa can make any appearance, at any time.

It has also taken us into a thirty-year residency at St. Louis's famed Venice Café, where every night is a combination of Christmas lights, Mardi Gras flair, and eye-popping absurdity. We've shared the Venice stage with Tiny Tim, Hank Rotten Jr., and Uncle Bill Green. The knucklehead meter is always pegged at the Venice.

Not only is Chris a spry, animated man, he's a very accomplished musician. He also knows every Christmas song in the book, as well as every polka, reggae, and classic rock song in all the other books.

Not only does "Indian" play his fiddle with abandon and flair, he can switch to his washboard, which has every scratch and sniff, bell and whistle, jangle and noise maker on it. The cacophony is wonderful.

The band can appear in many forms. Sometimes it's just the two of them. Believe me, they can still make enough racket for everyone.

When the Garbonzos start to play, no matter the size or shape of the band, no one can resist joining in. When I can make a gig, I automatically enlist. I love the lunacy and camaraderie.

There is no better avenue than the Garbonzos, for a cartoon character like Santa Claus. It is a marriage made at the North Pole. The two are a mug of warm ale and a jolly good time.

Fat & Funny

You can find the Garbonzos at https://www.facebook.com/**Garbonzos**

Remember, the gig is still the gig. It may be only a four-minute song at the end of a forty-minute show. It may be only a brief cameo in the middle of a video. The gig is still the gig.

Yes, folks, after all these years, I still get that rush. It's that rush that makes musicians play. It's that rush that makes actors act.

There's no business like show business. Ho, ho, ho, ho, ho.

19

You Are What You Eat

Rule 7: Do not eat at a Mexican restaurant before a Santa gig.

This may be one of the shorter chapters in the book, but it will definitely, beyond the shadow of a doubt, be the most important of them all.

Let's face it. If you're doing this Santa thing, you're an old guy. We've already established that. We're all old guys. We may not have our wits about us, but we still have our bodily functions (to varying degrees).

Bodily functions must be dealt with, not only for the two hours you're in the Santa suit. They must also be dealt with, for the other twenty-two hours of the day. For the sake of this essay, let's just focus on your time 'in the suit'.

I know what my innards are like. You should know what yours are like, too. We all should know what our innards are like.

I know what settles mine, and I know what sets them off. You should know this, as well. After all, we deal with them on an everyday, first-name basis.

You sure don't want your tummy yapping at you in the middle of a gig. You can cover up bad breath with that peppermint stick, you should have in your pocket. That mint is meant to refresh. It shouldn't have to cover up a Volcano Shrimp cocktail.

Precautions should be taken at all costs. A good idea is to always have a roll of antacids nearby. A quick gulp of a carbonated beverage, will also do the trick. Just don't belch in anyone's direction. Once again, peppermint stick.

We old guys may not be able to remember what we had for lunch, but we sure can tell when something's not agreeing with our gut.

I have always loved asparagus. I like the flavor and the crunch. I like them on my plate, sitting right next to a sizzling steak. It's too bad, asparagus doesn't like me. Unfortunately, a veggie omelet with asparagus before a gig, is a massive no-no.

Beer breath is beer breath. Beer farts are another thing. Beer farts are natural. Beer breath is a choice. *Bad Santa* is a funny movie. Shoot for a different kind of funny.

Don't let your beer breath get so bad, that the peppermint stick in your pocket can't fix it. For most old guys, this isn't a big deal. Most Santa gigs are in the daytime and you shouldn't be smelling like a gin mill in the daytime, anyway. (Okay, down from my soapbox).

Rule 8: There's a big difference between number 1 and number 2.

Before a gig, it is *always* wise to check out *exactly* where the bathroom is, in case you need to make the fifty-yard dash. This can be taken care of, quite easily. As you lumber about and meander to your spot, pay close attention to where the toilet is.

It's also not wise to guzzle water while you're sitting as Santa. You'll be much better off with a brief 'wet the whistle', than a frantic 'dash for the urinal'.

Take it easy. Relax. Gulping is not very courteous. It's also not very smart. Gently sip from your room-temperature cup. If you're like me, there's a cold, frosty guzzle awaiting in your sleigh.

Don't get me wrong. As a working musician, I've made many, many mad dashes for the urinal. It's not pretty. It's not fun. It can be a close shave. You live. You learn. It's called wisdom.

Eventually, everyone has to take a leak, even Santa. If you have to pee, you have to pee. That's just the way the human body is. There's no way around it. But find a way to do it, before your situation gets too critical. This is no big deal. Do not let it become one. It shouldn't be that hard to figure out.

If you find yourself with a situation, like a long line or an "out of order" sign, your porcelain dash could get tense. Most of the time, guys will just smile and let Santa jump to the head of the line. But if there are kids involved, Santa must wait.

If you bolt early enough and take care of business, you won't find yourself wincing, pinching, and fretting in line, and you can quickly get back out and onto your non-porcelain throne.

Zipping up is a welcomed sound, especially when you still have an hour of "ho, ho, ho" to go.

Rule 9: Coffee is a no-no.

Know which kinds of food and drink agree with you and which kinds to stay away from. Know which are soothers and which are triggers. Every adult should know this about themselves.

My wife has owned a coffee shop for the past two decades. I adore my cup of coffee. We both just love the stuff. But, before a gig, I must abstain and pay attention to my seventy-one-year-old innards.

(Rule 9 also applies to travel days in airports. There is nothing worse than standing in a long, early-morning line at airport security with a bad urge for the big purge.)

On travel days, as well as Santa gigs, coffee holds the same sway with me. Though I still have a wonderful relationship with the stuff, I must lay off. I don't like it much, but if I have to, I can make my way through a morning without my cup of joe. An adverse reaction can really be disastrous. All it takes is one close call to learn this lesson. Like I said, number two is different than number one.

I also love fruit. I love everything about fruit, especially bananas. I value their cleansing quality and inclusion in my daily life. I enjoy a fruit smoothie as much as the next guy. I also know, what makes my gut feel good now, might not make Santa's butt feel so good later.

Rule 10: Food and drink are important. Pay attention.

You should also know which foods effect your bodily aromas. Pay attention to these emanations. Aromas can linger, linger, and linger longer. The only things you can do, once they start are, 1) ignore the lingering and 2) hope nobody else notices.

Most adults are understanding. If it's not too obnoxious, they'll just turn the other nostril. Kids don't have the same filter. One outburst of "Eww!" can quickly dispense of any ambience. At that point, the reindeer is out of the bag.

Aromas come in two categories: 1) AB, above the belt and 2) BB, below the belt. Aromas from above the belt (a.k.a. B.O.) can permeate nicely, all throughout that big, fluffy coat you're wearing. Aromas from below the belt (a.k.a. oh, no) can also attach themselves nicely to those big, soft britches.

Sweaty feet should be kept in their boots at all times. Do not take your boots off until you are long ago and far away. Stinky feet can be quite offensive. Take no chances here.

The golden rule is: 1) try not to work up a sweat and 2) try not to fart too bad.

It can get very stuffy in that suit, so it's advantageous to have a stick of deodorant nearby. When you find a little lull in the action, a couple slaps of Old Spice should do the trick. A little dab'll do ya.

If things become too prevalent, a stretch and a stroll away from your area should disperse the curse. If that doesn't do the trick, a brisk walk around a wide circumference will have to be taken. It's your own damn fault. Remember the asparagus? You knew better.

We don't need to get into any gruesome, bathroom-crisis stories. Everyone's had them. No one likes to talk about them. We won't talk about them here, either. Just make sure your outtards make sure your innards are at bay.

Rule 11: Don't eat a chili dog at a gig. Cookies are okay.

You will be offered lots of things to eat. It's Christmastime. Food is everywhere. You can't get away from it. Folks love large, fancy, party spreads, and they're always generous with Santa. If you wish, you can partake. Once again, there are no written rules. But remember, you have your girlish figure to maintain.

I just never felt comfortable, dribbling barbecue sauce into my beard and down the front of my coat. If the food looks nice, I'll ask one of the hostesses to fix me a plate, for later. It always goes well with that cold, smooth beverage I have in my truck. I must keep my ghoulish figure, too.

Most of the rules above pertain here. But if there is asparagus on the table—well, you get the picture. Once again, trust your gut.

Cookies are different. They are important. Cookies have sugar and smell sweet. Cookies won't spoil your breath. They can be a nice part of your shtick.

When a child offers you a cookie, you cannot—I repeat, *you cannot*—refuse it. Whether you eat it or not, you must accept it and do so, graciously. A spurned cookie can lead to a sad, deflated child. Do not let this happen.

Make a big deal out of it. Emote. Take a nibble and mutter "mmm, mmm, mmm." Rub your belly and mutter "mmm, mmm, mmm." Every kid will smile. It'll work every time. I haven't seen a child yet, who hasn't been absolutely thrilled when Santa takes their cookie.

You can hold long conversations about cookies. You can make up short, little stories about cookies. You can muster elaborate tales about cookies. Cookies can also be used to end a visit. One of your more effective, go-to, end-of-visit cookie stories may go as follows:

> Santa: "Will you do me a favor when you go to bed on Christmas Eve?"
>
> Child: (nodding silently, moon-pie eyes)
>
> Santa: "What's your favorite cookie?"

Michael Supe Granda

Child: (says their favorite cookie)

Santa: "Wow. That's my favorite cookie, too" (no matter what the kid says).

Child: (smiles and giggles)

Santa: "Here's what I would like you to do, please. On Christmas Eve, before you go to bed, leave me only one cookie and only a half glass of milk. That's because I can't drink a whole glass—I don't have time—and we don't want to waste milk. Oh, yeah. One more thing. Will you leave some carrots for my reindeer?"

As I garner nods, I know I have connected with the child and then look to the parents. They're usually thrilled with the scene and entertained by the shtick. If things are frolicking, I can bloat my story with simple twists and silly turns. This only leads to more giggling.

Right before they walk off, I quickly and quietly engage the entire family. I draw them all close and whisper, "Remember. Only one cookie, only a half glass of milk, and some carrots." This will be the center of conversation around their dinner table every evening, until Christmas. As they stroll off, I know each child will mull my instructions with a fine-tooth comb. Yep, cookies are a valuable, flexible tool for Santa.

Then, when Santa's done, he can head to his truck, take off his suit, drink beer, and spill barbecue sauce all over himself.

Fat & Funny

Rule 11b: If you feel the slightest twinge, don't reach over and lift up a fat kid.

If you feel even the slightest twinge of anything abdominal, remember Newton's simple law of physics: "For every action, there is an equal and opposite reaction." You don't want any kind of opposite reaction. Opposite reactions can be catastrophic.

Let the kids jump around and jump into your lap. Just don't try to lift them. Don't lift anything. There is no room for a mistake here. There is also no room for a hernia.

Okay, that's enough. How much more is there to say about this sophomoric topic? Not much. You get the picture. Pay attention to your body. Like I said earlier, this may be the shortest chapter in the book. Now, you know why it's the most important.

Zip.

20
Out of the Suit

During the month of December, there are going to be times when you will be mistaken for Santa, and you won't be dressed as Santa. You won't even be thinking about Santa. It will happen when you least expect it.

Expect it at the grocery store. Expect it at the post office. Expect it on parking lots and in coffee shops. Expect it when you're wearing jeans and a sweatshirt, minding your own business.

It's no big deal. After all, you still do resemble him.

Folks don't really hound you, and they're not being pests. It's no big deal. It's always in good fun.

You become the lovable catcher's mitt of banter—and you'll hear plenty of it. You'll hear funny jokes and not-so-funny jokes. You'll hear knee-slapping wisecracks and good-natured profanity.

You can steer any interaction into any direction you want, and for as long as you want (or don't want). Most of the time, folks just want to give you a friendly smile, a wave, and a "Hey, Santa." Others just want a quick selfie and a little clever conversation. If I hear a wacky comment, my mind automatically defaults to 'wacky'. Then, I'll instantly slash back with, hopefully, a funny retort. Instant? Yes. Funny? Hope so.

That's just my nature. I can't help it. I will never ever pass up the chance for a sight gag, a slapstick bit, and a silly song. When the jokes start to fly, just let 'em rip.

Sometimes, you hit the mark. Other times, not so much. Sometimes, you hit the bull's-eye, while other times, you don't even hit the dartboard. But if you're a funny-minded guy (it's right there in the title of this book), you must trust your funny bone-to-mouth coordination. Let instinct take over and enjoy interacting with other goofy, creative people.

Some of the exchanges are quite funny and very witty. Not only do I enjoy this, I put it to good use, utilizing banter as exercise. Improvisation is a nice asset for this job. Plus, it's a fun street to walk down.

Another thing is your lid. Santa hats are very effective in cold weather. You'll see little old ladies wearing them. You'll see skinny, bald guys and kids wearing them. You'll see cashiers at the grocery store wearing them. Many folks wear them, just to keep their heads warm. After all, it is December.

Santa hats may be everywhere. If you don't resemble Santa, wearing one simply lets people know, you're in the holiday spirit. It's no big deal.

It is a big deal, though, if you do resemble Santa. If you resemble Santa *and* you're wearing a Santa hat, interaction is assured and instant. There will be times, even when you're just wearing a regular stocking cap, that you'll still be identified as him. It's no big deal. Have fun with it.

If you keep a twinkle in your eye, you can set yourself apart from all the other old guys, shuffling around with scruffy beards. If you're the twinkling type, people notice young hearts in old chests.

You'll garner smiles and comments from adults. Everyone

knows you by name. "Hey, Santa," is usually followed with, "I've been a good girl this year. I want a new Jeep." Wisecracking is essential.

Chucklers will chuckle and go on their merry way with holiday smiles. When an awestruck child recognizes *you* as *him*, just turn on *his* charm. It will warm your heart, as well as make their day.

One quiet Tuesday morning, which is Senior Day at my local grocery store, I slowly roamed the produce aisle, pushing my cart, planning menus, and picking out ingredients. Brenda Lee and Andy Williams sang Christmas tunes through the PA system in the store's ceiling. It was a warm, comforting environ. As I stood by the artichokes, a young, bearded man approached.

As he gingerly neared, I could tell he was a soft soul with a good heart and a sincere question. He informed me that his four-year-old daughter had spotted me around the corner and was insisting that I was him.

Even though, I was in regular clothes, she was excited. She had spotted Santa, and he was wearing a black beret, blue jeans, and a green muffler. She and her mother continued shopping, strolling along the breakfast cereal aisle. The little girl hadn't noticed that her daddy had snuck off.

He started with, "May I ask you a question?"

I replied, "Yes, you may."

He asked, "Do you get this often?"

I replied, "Yes, I do."

When he asked if I would nonchalantly meander by and greet his daughter, I replied, "Yes, I will. What's her name?"

"Her name is Lauryn," he said.

Fat & Funny

I've done this numerous times. I instructed him to head back to his family and I would meet them in the frozen food section in ten minutes.

I turned back to my artichokes, with a calm in the air and the voice of Harry Belafonte from on high. Then, I strolled to my frozen rendezvous.

As I slowly turned the corner of the long, empty aisle, I began picking out ice cream. Out of the corner of my eye, I could see the young family at the far end. Though, I didn't look up, I could almost hear her gasp. I paid no attention, as I casually shopped and made my way up the quiet aisle.

When we got close, I looked up from my shopping list and saw the child's beaming face. I acted surprised, as if I were the startled one. This put her at ease. Then, I laughed. "Ho, ho, hi, folks. How is everybody doing, today?"

Although I had picked up on the child's excitement, she was still a bit shy. So, I turned to her parents and struck up my usual, "Are you folks ready for Christmas?"

With each exchange, the child began to settle and come out of her shell. By the time I got to, "Do you have a tree?" she blasted all the way out. "Yes!" she blurted. "We have a beautiful tree with beautiful ornaments, and I made 'em at my school."

Then, she proceeded to fill me in on all the details of her tree, her puppy, her artwork, and her princess pillowcase. As I listened, I slowly opened the door, to grab some frozen waffles. I smiled and just let her talk. Her mother dabbed tearing eyes. Her father busted buttons. I enjoyed the warmth and family bond.

I waited for the little one to catch her breath. Then, I quickly asked, "What would you like for Christmas?" As she began running through her wish list, I was listening to Shirley Temple. I didn't let her ramble on too long, though. Mission was accomplished. She had talked to Santa, and Santa still had beer and pretzels to buy. When we went our separate ways, I was careful to avoid catching her eye again. I wanted *his* myth to remain intact.

I did see them once more, as they walked out the door. The little girl was still aflutter, agiggle, and agog. The joy I witnessed was well worth the five minutes it took, between buying Eggos, Budweiser, and Cherry Garcia.

My gig had gone well. It was a formal ordeal—three hours on a Saturday morning (11:00 a.m.–2:00 p.m.) at the Country Music Hall of Fame. At 11:01, I was talking to children. At 2:01, I was making a quick jaunt to Julie's coffee shop, where I could help her for a couple of hours, before my 5:00 evening gig.

When I left the hall, I took off my hat and coat. Because my next appearance was relatively soon, I decided to keep my trousers, suspenders, and boots on. This way, I could easily make it across town to the other soiree.

When I walked in, the lunch crowd had begun to thin. I walked in as *me*. As I began to wash dishes and wipe down counters, I was *me*. I enjoy being me, getting lost in small tasks. I like zoning out, oblivious to everything around me. When friends stopped by, I could easily dry my hands and shake theirs. Owning a coffee shop can really be friendly and fun.

Julie tapped me on the shoulder. She turned her back to the window and pointed to a young boy at a table in the food court, having lunch with his family. She said, "He's been staring at you for ten minutes. I think, he thinks you're really Santa." He couldn't have been five years old. I knew I had to visit.

Remember, even when you don't have your heavy coat on, you still resemble him. With only my pants, a gray T-shirt, black boots, and some red suspenders, it was time to turn on *his* charm.

Out of the corner of my eye, though I could see the excitement, I didn't rush right over. I could tell his family was still in the middle of their meal. They'd be sitting there, for a while.

I did pay attention, and Julie was right. I felt him. I saw him. The kid was staring holes in the back of my head.

I continued to piddle around the shop. When I noticed their emptied plates, I strolled out our doorway and stretched my arms, pretending to be *him*. I started to cluelessly meander toward them. When I caught his eye, I saw his exhilaration.

Then, I caught the attention of his folks, who knew what was going on. They knew what I was doing. With a tempered "Ho, ho, ho," I grabbed two cookies from Julie's counter, one for the boy and one for his infant sister. I slowly wandered to their table and flipped the switch on the little, jolly, wind-up toy.

I walked right up to the lad and handed him his dessert. I could tell the kid was speechless, so I began asking his father simple questions. After each one, I turned to the child, who was nibbling away. When the lad felt comfortable enough to start chattering, I turned my total attention to him. Then, I just let him loose. A-chatterin' he went.

After several minutes, the family began to collect their things. I wished them a happy holiday, ruffled the boy's hair, took a photo, excused myself, and walked off. They danced out the market door. I strolled back to Julie's.

The whole encounter took fewer than five minutes. Most encounters like this, take fewer than five minutes.

An hour later, I hopped back into my truck, pulled on my coat, tightened my belt, and dashed my way across town, for the evening.

For eleven years, Julie ran her coffee shop (Butter Cake Babe Coffee Cafe) in the Nashville Farmers' Market. For many of those holiday seasons, I sat outside her door, as Santa. December Saturdays in the market house were lovely and low-key. We had no giant throne. There were no plush, red velvet curtains. The tree was modest. We just wanted to thank our customers, with some cheer and a free photo.

Fat & Funny

There was very little pressure, and it was great fun. I enjoyed turning into *him*, just hanging around a coffee shop. There were no long lines. When I saw a family with kids approaching, I could easily stroll out of our little bubble, to our little blue table and sit in any of the chairs. Engaging kids and conjuring holiday spirit can be quite fulfilling.

While I sat and chatted with the youngsters, the grown-ups walked up to the window, to visit Julie. Returning with cups of warmth and butters of cake, we all focused and smiled for their cameras. Another happy customer. The smiles were as genuine as the day is real. Many, many friends stopped by for a spell, a chat, and a warm photo. We love every one of them.

One of our good customers, Peter Cooper, stopped by often. Several years earlier, as I was just beginning to hone my chops, I visited one of his Saturday morning neighborhood gatherings. Along with banjo player, Mark Horn, all four families had young children. While the kids gathered and frolicked upstairs, I snuck in Mark's front door.

The feeling was festive. The tree was lit. The children went out of their minds, when Santa magically appeared up the steps and began to play with them. We did our thing. Then, I magically disappeared. It was one of my first, full-blown appearances in my first, full-blown suit.

Peter knew a good Santa when he saw one. As entertainment editor for Nashville's daily newspaper, *The Tennessean*, he recognized entertainment value.

When he devoted one of his weekly columns to my wacky endeavor, he observed, "Basically, he just stops shaving every September, packs on some pastry-aided pounds, and waits for Santa to appear. Then, he sings, 'By the middle of November, I look like a rusty old can. But, by the first of December, I look like a jolly old man.'"

Though, the article didn't garner oodles of fame, it did lead directly to my gig at the Hall of Fame. When Peter accepted the head writer post at the hall, he moved from the paper to the museum.

He remembered what I did, and knew that I knew what I was doing. That December, he called, in a Friday-morning panic. Their regular Santa had fallen ill and wouldn't be able to make it in for this, the final weekend of their season.

When I happily agreed to bail out their Saturday and Sunday, he and his staff liked what I did. This has led to a wonderful, six-year tenure in the Grand Lobby of the Country Music Hall of Fame. Folks, this is the Rolls-Royce of gigs, and one I deeply cherish.

As the official 'old man of the hall', it may be safe to say that I've had my picture taken more times than any of the enshrinees, by a North Pole country mile.

For this gig, I make sure no one sees me out of costume. This is very important. When people go to Disney Land, they don't want to see a half-dressed Mickey Mouse, eating a ham sandwich and smoking a cigarette. When I arrive and walk in the back door, no one sees me as *me*. No one notices when *me* walks back out that same door, at the end of the day. When I'm done, part of *my* gig is to make *him* disappear.

There are tunnels, green rooms, wood shops, locker rooms, and bulletin boards. As I come and go, I don't need a security badge. You don't really need a security badge when you're Santa Claus.

This is a totally professional venue. I approach my gig the same way. We work well together. I give them a professional, three-hour show. Once again, the Court Jester is a legitimate occupation. It's a joy to work with professionals, in any line of work.

Michael Supe Granda

When you're *him*, you'll get recognized as *him*. When you're not *him*, you'll still get recognized as *him*. That might be *you* out of the suit, but that's *him* in the suit.

Elvis never had this luxury. When he wasn't in the suit, he was still Elvis. But never forget—Santa is still bigger than Elvis.

21
Flirting with Santa

Rule 13: Learn how to flirt.

As I've said before, every woman, every girl, every lady, every niña—no matter her age—loves Santa Claus. They love everything about Santa Claus. They love his jingle. They love his jangle. He jingles and jangles, just like them. They love getting their pictures taken with him. They want to snuggle and be cuddled by a big, fuzzy furball. They want to hold his hand. They like his fluffy beard. They like everything about Santa.

They want to tell Santa they've "been a good girl." They want to tell him what they want for Christmas. They also want to tell Santa they've "been a bad girl" and all about their personal problems and recent surgeries.

A lot of guys couldn't give a rat's ass about Santa Claus. I understand, completely. As you know, I'm not a Christmas geek. I'm more of a Christmas goob. I look at this, as just a gig. As a young lad, once I figured out his deal, I didn't pay much attention to him.

Every girl, though, adores him, and many like to flirt with him. Not every girl is going to, but if they do, be ready. Some will flirt in slim, subtle ways. Others will flirt with the subtlety of a jack hammer.

You must learn that it is possible to flirt in playful ways and that Santa knows playful ways. You must also remember, "For he's a jolly good fellow. Fa-la-la-la-la, la-la-la-la."

A couple of basic Santa rules about flirting: 1) Don't start the flirting, and 2) if the flirting comes, start playing volleyball.

When and if Cupid flings his arrow, just start improvising. Return their volley with a compliment about anything—their hair, their dresses, their shoes, their scarves, their earrings, their nose rings.

When and if the second arrow flies and the questions let off the accelerator, you know the flirting can stay cool, calm, and collected. If this happens, things should be fine. Innocent flirting can be lighthearted and funny.

But if the second shot gets dark and racy, usually from older gals, you must know how to diffuse the situation and steer conversation back toward the light. You can easily do this by *simply not taking the bait*. Then, you can just whisk them off down the line, out of the picture, and back into their lives.

It will benefit you, as Santa to learn the art of flirting. A little flirting isn't necessarily a bad thing. Flirting has been around since the beginning of time. Everyone has done it. This art of flirting may be fifteen minutes older than the oldest profession in the world.

It can make for interesting banter between a man and a woman, even if the man is Santa Claus. You might not feel like it. You might not want anything to do with a beard, a broad, and

Fat & Funny

a bunch of banter. But Santa does. It's his jolly, but it's your gig. Your gig will be over soon. Until then, jolly up a storm.

I can detect an approaching flirt from a mile away. I can see it, as it comes down the quiet hallway. I can see it, as it jumps off the noisy barstool. Whether it comes from a six-year-old with a button nose and a new sweater, or a sixty-six-year-old with an ex-husband and a trailer, there's no mistaking it.

I can see it all around me. Remember, Santa presides over a large area. He sees everything. It's more fun than watching cable TV.

I've also noticed that girls aren't the only ones who are adept at the art. They're just more subtle about it. Believe me. Boys flirt, too.

Boys pay no attention to me. I'm completely invisible to them. They don't want anything to do with me, but they want everything to do with the girls. I really like to just sit there and watch them flap and flop around.

It is really fun and funny to watch young boys flirt. Most of the time, they just lope around, punch each other in the arm, and act stupid. It's also entertaining, though slightly embarrassing, to see Gomer and Goober in front of a gaggle of gals. Most of the time, their gangling involves headlocks, wrestling stunts, karate moves, blabbermouths, and skinny arms.

Whoever first observed that girls mature faster than boys, is absolutely correct. The difference is noticeable and really, really funny to watch.

When little girls flirt, the innocence can be quite a lovely thing. They're excited about their snowflake purse and their reindeer pin, and they want to make sure Santa notices. As Santa, you *must* notice everything, even their socks. They love showing off their socks, which often match their scarves and the bows in their hair.

Many times, girls will take notice of the slight rouge I put on my nose and cheeks. It's chilly at the North Pole. My nose should look chilly. My cheeks should look rosy. We all huddle, scrunch our shoulders, and compare make-up tips. Girls like to talk about make-up and making up with boyfriends.

They like to whisper, and it's Santa's job to attentively listen to their every tidbit. When this happens, there won't be any blatant, ugly flirting. These small, brief, intimate visits can be wonderfully fun. Plus, what happens in Santa's ear, stays in Santa's ear.

You can elongate any visit you want, for as long as you want. All you have to do is issue another compliment about another adornment. Let them do all the talking. Girls like to talk. When they do, some can really go to town. You just listen and look up at the clock on the wall.

It is cute to watch little girls paw at the ground, swing their arms around, and twinkle. Some will burst into song, while some will mumble along. Sing along with the singers, but make sure the shy kids are also comfortable enough to speak up and speak out.

Sometimes, when older gals flirt, it can be a train wreck. Not only do you have to deal with lewder language, you have to deal with the aroma of Marlboro Lights and malt liquor. Just like younger girls, older gals like to talk too. They'll talk your ear off.

Plus, many of them like to talk really raspy and raspy loud. They want to make sure everyone in the vicinity hears their hard-luck stories. Luckily, you're Santa Claus and, if need be,

Fat & Funny

you can quickly get to the shuffling off and whisking away part of the show.

Many of these gals live alone with their televisions, and they just want to talk to somebody. You just happen to be that certain somebody. Older men live this way too; it's not a gender thing. Older men don't walk up and tell me all their secrets.

Little girls like to hold their hands up to the mouths and meekly mumble through their fingers. They want you to hear all about their Christmas trees and their new puppies. Older gals like to get right to the point. They want you to hear all about their horrible romances, their medical problems, and their pathetic sex lives. The scariest part of this equation is, you and she are about the same age, and Santa is looking pretty tasty.

Even though you are *him*, remember, you're not really him. Santa might be the man of their dreams. You are not and believe me, you don't want to be. Do not take their phone numbers. Immediately forget all phone numbers. Do not take notes from them. Wad up the papers and discard them as soon as they leave. Definitely, definitely, definitely do not take motel room keys.

If they want to blow off steam and blow in your ear, blow them off. You must learn how to make absolute zero contact. You don't want them, following *him* to *your* house. You also don't want any restraining orders.

Little, little girls really don't know what they're doing yet. Still, it's kinda there and it's still kinda fun to watch. They're just starting to attain abilities. The flirting is in its infancy.

As they get a little older, you can see them begin to hone the craft. The flirting gets craftier.

As they get a little older, you can see them using finer sandpaper. The flirting gets smoother.

As they get a little older, you can see that life has tossed them around the ring. The flirting gets crazier.

As they get a little older, you can field wide ranges of emotions, flying in every direction. The flirting gets crasser.

Then, you can see them well down that yellow brick road. The flirting gets desperate.

I'm not telling you what to do on this topic. Once you're out of the suit, you're on your own. Once you're out of the suit, you can come down any chimney you want. While you're in the suit, you're on the clock (if that's how you are approaching all this).

While you're in the suit, you will be best served, if you keep in mind: 1) this is still a gig, 2) this crazy cast of characters are only bit players shuffling across your stage, and 3) the show will soon be over.

You've seen flirting in many shapes and sizes. You've seen it happy. You've seen it sad. You've seen it lovely, and you've seen it ugly. You've seen it demure. You've seen it blatant. You will see it all, my friend. Be a good judge.

22
The Last Waltz

Well, you made it. Here you are. You're getting ready to suit up for the last gig of the year. In a few hours, you'll be getting ready to take the suit off for the last time, too. It's late December, and this ends your busy (or, not-so-busy) schedule that started around Thanksgiving.

There are three, equally important scenes to this, the final act:

Scene 1: Putting the suit on for the last time (about six o'clock).

Scene 2: Taking the suit off for the last time (about nine o'clock).

Scene 3: Stashing the suit for next year (tomorrow morning).

Around October, the calls began to come in and you began scheduling your season. Then, in late November, you started gigging the season away. One of the most important aspects of this whole equation took place eleven months ago. This was very apparent at the beginning of this season.

The success of the 'November opening' of your Santa suitcase is in direct correlation to the last 'January closing' of your Santa suitcase. This initial opening is always a big moment. You *must* think about next year, when you take off the sweaty suit for the last time this year.

I breathe a sigh of relief at the end of each season. Complete with a sense of accomplishment and a tumbler of tequila, my mind turns to recollected thoughts of the past month, the musings, and these essays. Then, there are all the trinkets and mementos you've gathered.

Kick back. You just started your eleven-month vacation. Off to the North Pole or South Pacific, you go. On, Dancer. On, Prancer. On, Coconut.

Once again—and I hate to keep harping on this—the most important thing to heed is, "A wet Santa suit can rival a wet dog." You don't want to smell like a wet dog. You don't want to smell like a wet anything. You also don't want to have to buy a whole new suit next year.

I carry a large, green, Ward-Cleaveresque suitcase for all the accoutrements. Get yourself a hefty, handy case of any kind and any color. You can find a good one at the thrift store for a few bucks. Make sure it's sturdy enough to tote around quickly and large enough to easily carry everything.

It must be versatile, but you must not overcram it with stuff. After a gig, if Santa needs to quickly scoot off to another gig, you don't want to be cramming and jamming and struggling around.

There are a few common-sense rules, you should adhere to. Over the month, you'll accumulate lots of little things, children have given you—the cutest, coolest, and cuddliest things. You have collected letters, pictures, drawings, ornaments, trinkets, toys, and chocolate bars.

They've given you cookies. (Don't forget the cookies.) Don't leave cookies in the bottom of your case. (Double-check for cookies in the bottom of your case.) A forgotten box of candy canes? Fugheddaboudit. (No, don't forget about it.)

Do not leave any kind of food item in your suitcase! Ants and bugs love melted chocolate kisses. Mice will tear right into a bag of cookies. Sticky candy canes will do a bang-up job on your fluffy coat.

In November, like every November, your calendar began filling with names, places, times, addresses, logistics, and cell phone numbers. (You *will* need a cell phone.)

All season long, you flitted about town, from gig to shining gig. Now, Christmas is nigh and your calendar is filled with scratched-off dates. One by one, you made every 8:00 a.m. gig. You made every 8:00 p.m. gig. You made every 9:30 a.m., 10:15 a.m., 2:30 p.m., and 6:45 p.m. gig.

When you started your run, Christmas Day was still a month away. The air crackled with anticipation. Now, as you finish, the big day is here. It may even be tomorrow. I've done quite a few Christmas Eve gigs. I don't mind. Rich uncles know that the price goes up for this day. They don't mind, either. Plus, I've never minded working on my birthday.

On top of all this, the sense of accomplishment is magnificent, like closing night of a successful theater run. Actually, it's exactly like closing night of a successful run - your one-man show. Sighs are sighed. You ride off into the sunset.

This past November, you opened your suitcase for the first time in eleven months. Hopefully, when you opened it, it didn't smell like Shaquille # 5. Hopefully, last January, when you packed it all away, you took precautions. This year, you'll need to take those same precautions.

Tomorrow, after this last gig, you can take the entire shooting match to the dry cleaners. After a thorough cleaning, it will return to its fluffy fireball of red. Let everything completely air out for several days (better safe than sorry). Wait for a brilliant, arid, sunny afternoon, before you put things back into hibernation (the back of your closet). You'll thank yourself (and me) in eleven months.

It's been a nice year. For Santa, every year is a nice year. You worked the amount you wanted to work. Some guys like to work - a lot. Others just don't. Some guys like to really book up their calendars. Other guys consider two appearances a season to be a heavy load.

Fat & Funny

This is your call. It has always been and always will be your call. There is no minimum amount of mandatory gigs you must do. You can cram as many as you want into a day. If you don't, you won't lose your Santa license. You don't have to fulfill any kind of gig quota. It's a beautiful thing.

You should feel a sense of melancholy when you "Santa up" for last time of the year. Not only have you stashed a few coins, you've strewn massive amounts of joy, along the way. You have laughed to the high heavens. On several occasions, your eyes have teared up, too. With all the goodwill you've spread to folks young and old, the jingle in your stocking is icing on your cake.

When I was young, I saw my father use this same approach. In his spare time, he became a baseball umpire, and a very good one. He took it quite seriously. It became a legitimate second job, and he treated it as such. Umpires got paid twelve dollars a game. His two games a day, turned into three nights a week, which turned into five games over the span of a weekend tournament. He did quite well at his side gig.

He umpired hundreds and hundreds of games. He would just take that extra cash, fold it up, and stick it in his back pocket. Then, we all went out for ice cream. Every summer was consumed with baseball. We never went hunting. We never went fishing. I was a sandlot kid. I've been to 12,608 baseball games and can't wait to see another one.

I treat my side gig with his same reverence and disciplines: 1) "Play ball," 2) "Ho, ho, ho," and 3) "The show must go on."

For the past month, you've paid close attention to your suit. You have to pay close attention to your suit. *You must at all times pay close attention to your suit.* It's an absolute requirement. Your suit is everything.

After each appearance, take stock of what needs attention, what needs replenishing, what needs repairing, and what needs laundering. If you need to tend to something, tend to it immediately. Do not dawdle.

Like a broken guitar string or a busted drumhead, don't wait until the last minute to replace it. That next last minute may turn into a disastrous panic. You don't need that. Santa doesn't need that. When Santa gets to his gig and gets ready to hit his downbeat, he doesn't want you, fumbling and scrambling around, trying to fix something.

If you're a carpenter, you respect your hammer. If you're a drummer, you respect your drum stick. If you're a Santa, you respect that big, fluffy suit. Make sure it stays fluffy next hour, next week, and next year.

Before every gig, go down your checklist. Write out an actual list, and check it thrice. You must make sure you have everything, *everything* on the sleigh. It is beyond embarrassing to get to an appearance and realize you forgot your hat and your gloves. I've done it. It is not fun. Most of us good ol' boys don't have such good memories, anyway. Cover your ass, guys.

Because of this, make your list and check it. Let's all sing it to the tune of "The Twelve Days of Christmas": 1) hat, 2) coat, 3) belt, 4) boots, 5) pants, 6) suspenders, 7) jingle bell, 8) twinkle, 9) glasses, 10) gloves, 11) gloves, 12) gloves, 13) breath mint.

For the past four weeks, you've hung your damp coat on hangers over air vents. Your sweaty hat has also dangled by its tuft over the same vents. Sweaty pants have been draped over couches (see the chapter on beer farts), and gloves have been laundered over and over (unless you've invested in multiple pairs). Boots have been shined (optional). For the past month, your living room has resembled Picasso's studio, with Gaudi splotches of red, splattered and scattered everywhere.

Everything must be dried *completely*. You don't want to leave anything damp, limp, and laying in a lump, overnight. In music lingo, musicians carry their axe. In Santa lingo, your suit is your axe. Treat your tools with respect. I cannot stress this enough.

You just did your last gig, a short, quiet, early-evening, low-key family affair. Beside a Norman Rockwell fireplace and 2.2 children, no one got too rambunctious, too out of hand, or too loud—except for a wee bit of squealing.

The Christmas season is also in its final, subduing stages. Those drunken, drag-out affairs of early December are replaced by calmer, more intimate gatherings. December's hysteria is tired.

Plus, it's almost over. It's closing night, just like any other closing night. Treat it as such. Remember, this is still an acting gig. Here's a script you can try on for your swan song.

> You spruce up in the car.
> You jolly up in the dark.
> You knock on the door.
> The lights come on.
> The curtain goes up.
> The children scream.
> You smile for the cameras.
> You shake everyone's hand.
> Aunt Isabella hands you her magic envelope.

Michael Supe Granda

The curtain comes down.
You're back in your car.
You're home in time for the news.
I'm home in time for a birthday beer.
Merry Christmas and Hey, Skol.

23
Epilogue

So, there you have it—stories and jokes about being a Santa Claus. If you really want to be one, it's ridiculously easy. These pages just described what an easy and entertaining path it has been for me. But if you really want, you can easily navigate his road to the North Pole.

So, there you have it—the story behind the main man and the story of being the myth of the main man. Sometimes, being mythical can be fun.

So, there you have it—the rest of the story. In days of yore, Santa may have been a figment of somebody's fertile imagination. But today, he is still very real and *very* important to many folks, especially young folks. He also holds a special place in the hearts of adults who cherish his occupancy.

So, there you have it—a good way for an old, fat guy to make a little extra cash for his stocking stash. All you need is time on your hands. Old guys, admit it. You got time on your hands.

So, there you have it.

What else can I say about being a good Santa? Oh, yeah. If you're an old, happy hippy, there's good news for you. Old, happy hippies make really nice Santas. All you have to do is be fat and funny.

Good luck, have fun, and ho, ho, ho.

Photo Credits

vii – Dog People
xi – St. Louis, 1953
1 – Ford White Photography
8 – private collection
11 – Julie Granda
16 – private collection
29 – private collection
33 – private collection
38 – private collection
52 – Stacie Huckeba
121 – Julie Granda
125 – courtesy Tennessee Titans
134 – Jamie Rubin
136 – Micky Dobo
143 – Casey Lutton
145 – Casey Lutton
145 – Kevin Wisniewski
146 – Scott McEwen
166 – Julie Granda
167 – Steve Harman
168 – Mark Horn
168 – Mark Horn
177 – Stacie Huckeba
185 – Ford White Photography
189 – Madison Thorn

About the Author

On Sunday, February 9, 1964, when St. Louis native Michael Supe Granda saw the Beatles appear on the *Ed Sullivan Show*, he immediately knew what he would do for the rest of his life. The very next day, he got a guitar, acquired tunnel vision, taught himself to play, started a band, and began gigging everywhere he could. He still gigs as often as he can.

Although his early combos made nary a dent on the local scene, he spent his entire high school career hibernating and honing musical skills. In 1969, when he went to Springfield, Missouri, for college, he sought and found like-minded musicians, artists, and bohemians to make merry music and perform with. He found them, quickly.

As cofounder of the seminal seventies country-rock group the Ozark Mountain Daredevils, his passions have taken him onto the radio, onto television, into videos, into nightclubs and onto festival stages around the world. One of the most recent stages is the red velvet throne he sits upon, portraying Santa.

At seventy-one, he still actively records and performs with the Ozarks, now into their fiftieth year, as well as his numerous side projects (Silly Grandpa, Supe and the Sandwiches, the Garbonzos, Mark & Mike). He lives in Nashville, TN, where he's resided for the past thirty years, writing, recording, growing tomatoes and basil, and tending to his small record label/publishing company, Missouri Mule Music.

Along with his nine solo discs of original material, his songs have been recorded by Chet Atkins, Augie Meyers, Walter Egan, Dr. Demento, the Dog People, and Rockpile's Billy Bremner.

He's appeared in videos by Tom Mason, Collin Raye, Trisha Yearwood and BR549.

Fat and Funny is his second self-published book, following his 2008 tome *It Shined: The Saga of the Ozark Mountain Daredevils*.